THE STREETCARS OF WINNIPEG
OUR FORGOTTEN HERITAGE

FriesenPress

Suite 300 - 990 Fort St
Victoria, BC, Canada, V8V 3K2
www.friesenpress.com

Copyright © 2015 by Brian K. Darragh
First Edition — 2015

Cover photo: William E. Robertson photo from Winnipeg Transit Photo Archive Collection. Cover designed by Sylvie Desjarlais CGD

All rights reserved.

No part of this publication may be reproduced in any form, or by any means, electronic or mechanical, including photocopying, recording, or any information browsing, storage, or retrieval system, without permission in writing from the publisher.

ISBN
978-1-4602-4652-8 (Hardcover)
978-1-4602-4653-5 (Paperback)
978-1-4602-4654-2 (eBook)

1. Transportation

Distributed to the trade by The Ingram Book Company

———— OUT OF SIGHT - OUT OF MIND ————

BRIAN K. DARRAGH

To TED DARRAGH

Brian K. Darragh

Dedication

I would like to dedicate this book to our daughter Charlene who spent countless hours working with the information and pictures that I had acquired over the years so that my story could be told in a way I envisioned it.

Acknowledgements

To those knowledgeable persons whose involvement in this project has been ongoing- I am greatly indebted. This book would never have been published without your participation.

About 90 percent of the 80 or more pictures in the book were taken between the early 1880's to 1955. Many of these pictures have been preserved in various archive collections, unfortunately the one that took that picture is not always mentioned. Having these photographs in the book is a great help, because you are reading about something that happened long before your time.

Likewise the vast majority of the written information comes from previously written books about Winnipeg Streetcars. The oldest one is, "The History Of Transportation in Winnipeg". It was written by Walter E. Bradley in 1958-59. Mr. Bradley came out from England in 1918. He then became a conductor on the Winnipeg Electric Railway and eventually worked his way up to Transportation Manager in the 1950's. He gave a very detailed description of Transit history from 1882 to 1955, with dates of new transit routes started and an inventory of the streetcars and rolling stock.

In 1971 Herbert W. Blake wrote 2 books "The Era of Streetcars in Winnipeg 1881 to 1955", and "The Era of Interurbans in Winnipeg 1902 to 1939". Information from these sources was a great help to procure all this information from the past.

The day I retired from Transit after 38 years of service July 31st 1992, the Company as a departing gift that last day gave me a copy of John Baker's book "Winnipeg's Electric Transit", (The story of Winnipeg's streetcars and trolley buses). As the last employee in the system that had operated a streetcar, maybe they had a feeling that some day I would write about them! This book has been one of my treasured gifts over my 22 years of retirement and I have consulted it thousands of times to check on some streetcar or electric trolley information. There is a chapter in my book about John Baker's book and quite frankly, my book could never have been written without Baker's one to call on. I particularly thank the Baker family for allowing me access to use their collection of information and photos.

Moving on to the present era, there are a number of people to thank for their support. My family of course including my wife Carol who sometimes had to listen to my frustration about something in the book's production that had hit a snag. Ms. Cindy Tugwell, Executive Director of Heritage Winnipeg, knows about my project, has provided information and has given encouragement in my pursuit of this project. She has also been quite involved with the task of trying to get our lone streetcar rebuilt - #356 in the Via Station Museum. It is now over 100 years old. The Archives of Manitoba was very helpful in assisting us to locate photos and to cite the appropriate sources. We appreciate their time and wealth of knowledge.

David McDowell, has been on the Heritage Streetcar Committee for many years. In fact about 10 years ago he was the one suggesting I write a book on them. He assisted in some preliminary editing of my early chapters.

I am thankful for the artistic expertise of Sylvie Desjarlais who created the front cover of my book. I appreciate her time and energy spent on this.

Gordon Sinclair has mentioned my forthcoming book in The Winnipeg Free Press. He has also sent some streetcar articles from the paper's archives as a source of information that helped to clarify and add depth in areas of the book. Ironically enough, Gord rode with me in my last week of work in 1992 and wrote an article outlining my days on the streetcar. Who knew we would go on to have a connection?

I am grateful to Christine Whiteside from Friesen Press for her time in answering endless questions and clarifying information along this journey. She has shown so much patience as we go through this process. Thanks is also expressed to the editing team at Friesen for their expertise in assisting me to create my story the best way possible.

But my good friend Steven Stothers has made a major contribution to my project. Steven wasn't even born till after the streetcars left, but in the last 10 or 12 years he has become very involved with their history. He has also bought the rights to a considerable amount of streetcar negatives and slides taken years ago and has offered those photo rights for my book for which I am grateful. I can't thank him enough for his efforts.

I am so fortunate to have access to all these pictures and printed material some of it going back nearly 130 years, that's where our daughter Charlene comes in. Charlene has put in countless hours on the computer rearranging paragraphs, moving pictures, editing, checking spelling and sentences, suggesting take outs and additions. My heart felt thanks Charlene.

Publishing this book has brought back a lot of memories over the past 60 years and hundreds of facial images of transit members now long gone. In 5 to 7 years the handful of us that are left will join them. Three generations born since 1955 should be made aware of "The Streetcars of Winnipeg Our Forgotten Heritage" out of site, maybe not out of mind.

It's Winnipeg's 150th anniversary in 2023, how about getting streetcar 356 on track then?

Preface

Ding ding.... Ding ding.

Do you remember the clang of the bell and the clatter of the wheels as one of Winnipeg's swaying streetcars rumbled down a portion of our 120 miles of streetcar track on its way downtown? If so, you had to have been in Winnipeg sometime during the first six decades of the last century (1900 - 1955) and be over 60 years of age, as the final streetcar reluctantly passed through Portage and Main on September 19, 1955 after 73 years of streetcar service.

You can conclude by adding those almost 60 years onto the age that an employee was at the time the cars ceased running so one can see that the few of us who are left are in our late 80s to mid-90s. So, in five to seven years' time, none of us will be around to pass on verbal information such as you will find in this book.

THE STREETCARS OF WINNIPEG

Former Minneapolis Car #814 in safety island on Portage Avenue, Winnipeg 1940. Library and Archives Canada/ Ronny Jaques Photo; copyright: expired. Archival reference no. R3133-1468-6-E MIKAN no 4328408

Streetcar 380 operated by author circa 1954. Steven Stothers collection

As a former Winnipeg streetcar and bus operator for 38 years, now into my third decade of retirement, my purpose

OUR FORGOTTEN HERITAGE

in publishing this book is to inform those born after 1950 about our streetcar heritage.

John Baker wrote the last published book on Winnipeg streetcars, *Winnipeg's Electric Transit: The Story of Winnipeg's Streetcars and Trolley Buses*, over 30 years ago (1982); it has been out of print for 25 years.

In those almost 60 years, three generations (children, grandchildren, and in some cases great-grandchildren) have little or no knowledge of Winnipeg's streetcar system, which began operation in 1882—over 35 years before the first four transit buses appeared in 1918.

By 1912 the streetcars were providing transportation to 150,000 residents and had helped build Winnipeg up to be Canada's third largest city. (At the time of writing Winnipeg challenged Hamilton for eighth spot.)

Streetcars served the city for 18 years before the first automobile (such as it was—a buggy minus the horse) arrived. After the T. Eaton Co. store opened in 1905, the only public transit to provide service to the stores for the next 13 years was the streetcars.

This streetcar system didn't just serve Winnipeg. An elongated (about 60 feet long) streetcar called an Interurban ran on tracks and was also powered by electricity; it was used to service Stonewall, Headingley, and Selkirk, Manitoba.

Over half of our Winnipeg streetcars were built right here in our city and in our final year (1955) Winnipeg Transit operated cars that were from 35 to 45 years old, along with its two newest cars, which were built here in 1928–'29. (Now we think we are doing well if we get 20 years out of a $400,000 bus!)

In 1873 Winnipeg became a city with a mere 1,869 residents; in 2023 the city will celebrate 150 years. Streetcars ran here for almost half that time and at the time of this writing Winnipeg had a population of 700,000 citizens. It leaves one to wonder what size Winnipeg would have been if the streetcars had never arrived.

In all likelihood you weren't part of this historic journey, so come along with me and I'll tell you all about it.

Interurban car #6 poses with Trailer #18. June 14, 1929 taken in Fort Rouge yards in Winnipeg Winnipeg. Transit Photo Collection - Stan Styles Photo

Introduction

A FARM BOY ADJUSTS TO CITY LIFE

For the first four-and-a-half years of my life we lived in Winnipeg—Mother, Dad, and myself. Then in 1933, in the middle of "The Dirty Thirties," we took up farming about 100 miles west of Winnipeg near a small community called Keyes, just west of Gladstone. For city slickers with no farm experience, this presented an entirely different lifestyle, but at least we had a garden and farm meat to eat and a roof over our heads. Unfortunately, the roof on the old house leaked like a sieve every time it rained and after putting up with it for a few years we tore the old house down. With the help of a few neighbors, we built a new one from the lumber salvaged from the old. However, this required living in a 14' by 14' tent for six months during the dismantling and reconstruction of the new house. In the summer the mosquitoes had a field day with us and in the last 10 days in the tent we had to sweep the fresh snow off the beds a couple of times before it melted.

When we moved into the shell of our new house on November 4, it was one big 24 foot by 20 foot room. Half of the windows weren't installed the first night, but once we got the cook stove and heater in place and had a nice warm fire going, after all those months in a tent it felt like a palace! The fact that we didn't have a car, radio, telephone, plumbing, or electricity for the next few years didn't seem to matter that night. (But those farm experiences are material for another book, perhaps sometime in the future should the opportunity arise.)

As a young child I was always fascinated by streetcars and remember being on them a couple of times when we lived in the city. Later, as a teenager and young adult, on occasional visits to the city I took a keen interest in them. After living on the farm for 21 years when I reached my mid-twenties I could see that the financial gains and opportunities of farming on a long-term basis were very limited in our area. The fact that the girl I was dating (and who would later become my wife) had moved to Winnipeg provided another incentive to move to the city. After being used to an outdoor life on the farm, I couldn't see myself working in a building or sitting inside an office for eight hours a day. My future wife suggested I try driving streetcars—it was somewhat of an outside job, and I had a passion for them, much as many young boys used to have a passion for steam trains. So, after living with my parents for the first 25 years of my life, I cut the apron strings and moved to Winnipeg.

In April 1954 I put all my worldly possessions in the trunk of my 1947 Mercury five-passenger coupe and headed for Winnipeg. Two weeks earlier I had made a trip up and had an interview, and, with beginners luck, they were in the process of hiring around 80 drivers that year. I would be in the first half-dozen of that group. I didn't realize it at the time, but down the road it would give me a much higher seniority than if I had been near the bottom of the list. Again, luck was on my side. Of those 80 men they only gave streetcar training to the first 20. They said that was all the operators for streetcars that they needed, as the cars would be gone in a year and a half. I wouldn't have had that chance had I not been in the first 20 drivers hired.

Arriving in Winnipeg on Good Friday gave me two days to find room and board before starting my new job the following Monday. I had officially left the somewhat tranquil life of the farm for a faster, busier, noisy life in the city. I wondered, after living my entire life with my parents up to that point, what I would encounter in this new lifestyle. Again someone was looking after me. After checking out a few room and board options, I found the ultimate place with a lady by the name of Mrs. Crawley on Home Street. The name of the street was appropriate, as it would soon very much be home to me.

Mrs. Crawley took in a couple of University students as well, but I had my own room and, of course, we shared the bathroom.

As a streetcar operator I had some weird hours. Sometimes I would have hours on both day shift and also be on the spare board, so I never knew what hours I would have for the week. Breakfasts and supper meals were included in the rent, but sometimes I needed to have breakfast at 4.30 a.m. Those mornings were early ones as I had to catch the 5 a.m. streetcar to the barns, and I didn't get home for supper until after 6.30 p.m. I used to tell Mrs. Crawley that it was no problem for me to make my own breakfast as long as she didn't mind me going into her fridge. (Cereal, toast, and tea aren't that hard to make!) But on the average, two or three times a week, if I was on the day shift, she would get up about 4.15 a.m. and make me breakfast! I told her this wasn't necessary but she always had some excuse. "Oh I wanted to get an early start on my washing." Or, "I remembered I hadn't taken something out of the freezer for supper." I knew it wasn't that important—she was just the type of person who liked to do things for people. Of course, when I was on the night shift and didn't come home until after 2 a.m., she would try and keep the house quiet in the morning while I slept. She was like a second mother to me and I was so lucky to find someone like that after leaving home to get involved in a new environment, and it gave me a great start on the next 38 years of my life. I stayed with her for the next 17 months until I got married, but I will always remember her kindness and compassion.

Chapter One

ROADS TO RAILS AND HORSES' TAILS

Manitoba became a province in 1870 and Winnipeg became a city on November 8, 1873. Outside of the first two railways that entered the city—the one from St. Paul, Minnesota arrived on December 7, 1878, and the Continental CPR from eastern Canada appeared in 1885, nothing helped the rapid growth and expansion of our city more than the Winnipeg streetcars.

Manitoba was one of five Canadian provinces that had horsecars, the precursors to streetcars. These single-horse-drawn cars began service on October 21, 1882, when Winnipeg's population was around 8,000 people.

The John Stephenson Company of New York built the first horsecars. Mr. Stephenson originally from Ireland, had the distinction of building the first horsecars for the city of New York when that city became the first city in the world to operate a horse-drawn streetcar service, beginning November 14, 1832.

Winnipeg horsecar on muddy Main Street in the early 1880s. Winnipeg Transit Photo Archive Collection

Winnipeg's horsecars continued for nearly 12 years and overlapped with the beginning of the early electric cars by more than three years. They were phased out by May 11, 1894. By that time the city had grown to nearly 40,000 people. Initially there were four cars and 20 horses, but by 1894 this had grown to 20 cars and over 80 horses.

The adoption of horsecars was a benefit to Winnipeg in many ways. The rail track that was laid on Main Street for the cars consisted of long timbers with cross ties laid over them to which 25-pound rails (25 pounds per lineal yard) were fastened. Electric cars were much heavier and required rails that were 60 to 90 pounds per yard. The horsecar track originally started on Main Street at Assiniboine heading north to the CPR crossing at Higgins Avenue.

The following year, when more horsecars arrived, tracks were extended along Portage Avenue to Kennedy Street and continued south to the Legislative Buildings at Kennedy and Broadway. Rails were also laid north of Higgins Avenue up Main Street to St. John's Avenue. For some time the track north of Higgins to St. John's Avenue was isolated due to the fact there was no track to allow the horsecars from south Main Street to cross over the CPR track at Higgins. So, it was timed that when a car from south Main Street arrived at Higgins Ave., passengers would get out and walk across the CPR track to a waiting horsecar that would take them to the end of the line at St. John's Avenue. This system also worked in reverse. No transfers were needed, as the waiting drivers saw passengers leaving the other car.

The construction of a "diamond" over the CPR tracks that crossed Main Street provided a brief solution to this delay. This crisscross track design, embedded in the track in 1898, allowed service from downtown up to St. John's Avenue to run uninterrupted and people no longer had to stop at one side and walk over. This situation was more formally addressed with the future CPR subway, constructed in 1904. This allowed train and car travel to occur simultaneously, without interruption to either. Service then continued seamlessly and without interruption up to St. John's Avenue and to the north and south ends of the city.

THE STREETCARS OF WINNIPEG

**Higgins underpass for streetcars – circa 1940 -
Winnipeg Transit Photo Archive Collection**

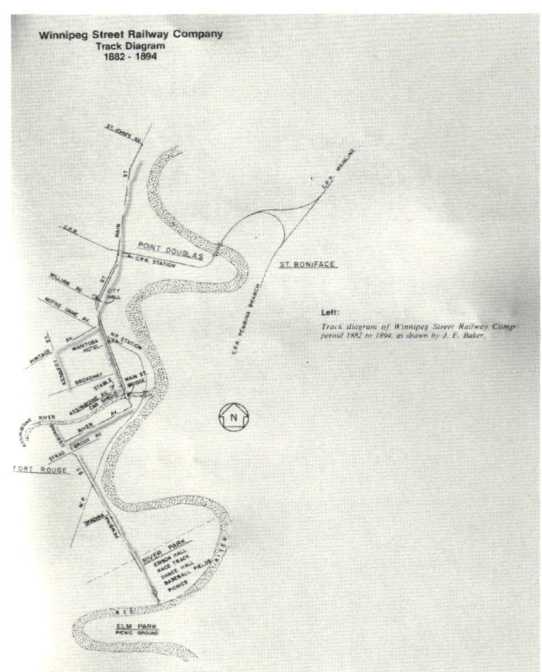

**Horse Cars Routes
Electric Car Service Routes Winnipeg Street Railway
Company Track Diagram 1882 – 1894; drawing by J. E.
Baker, Winnipeg's Electric Transit, p. 13. Highlighted
areas are horsecar and electric car service routes.**

OUR FORGOTTEN HERITAGE

In the early 1880s there were very few board sidewalks in Winnipeg. Paths of mud were the only option for navigating the early streets of Winnipeg. Likewise, after a rain the streets were quagmires of muck and gumbo and high rubber boots were needed to walk down the street. Residents soon discovered that by walking down the timbered rail track they could stay reasonably dry and devoid of mud. The farmers and tradespeople soon discovered that their teams of horses could pull their heavy loads much easier on the timbered base between the rails than in the slimy gumbo of the streets. This frustrated the drivers of the horsecars, who would normally travel much faster than the heavily loaded wagons of the farmers and tradespeople and presented yet one more challenge to the transportation system.

Horsecar on muddy Main Street, Spring 1884 H.W. Blake Collection

The horsecars were 16 feet long with open vestibules on either end. The driver stood out side on an open platform with a waist-high partition that was there to ward off the dirt kicked up by the horse's feet. A curved overhang from the roof extended partway over the driver's head, but still left him exposed to summer thunderstorms and winter blizzards. For his devotion to duty under these conditions he was paid 12 - 14 cents an hour and worked a 10½-hour shift six days per week. This would amount to about $35 a month for 25 days of work. With today's standards of safety and scrutinized working conditions, can you imagine working in such challenging circumstances for so little?

In the first year of operation, streetcar fares were a mere five cents a ride, but rose to 10 cents some months later. Those buying a strip or book of tickets found the rides to be a little cheaper. For a while "workman's tickets" could be purchased for three cents each but could only be used during specified morning and evening rush hours by those going to work.

In these early days there was no snow clearing equipment other than men with shovels. The city preferred to leave the snow on the streets all winter to make better sleighing for customers; as the ground was frozen, the streets could still be used. Albert W. Austin, the head of the Winnipeg Street Railway Company, adapted to the conditions by putting the body of the horsecars on sleighs and charged a little lower fare. They tried to maintain the same route, however, in the early spring before the snow melted away the street would get soft and some parts of it would become bare. Instead of two horses, four were needed to pull the sleighs through the snowless areas of the streets. As soon as the rails were clear in the spring, the body of the car would be placed back on the wheels.

**A horsecar equipped for winter service, circa 1882;
Winnipeg Transit Photo Archives Collection**

A few other logistical issues were similarly sorted out. In the beginning, since the track did not loop around at the end of the line as it did with the electric cars, and with the car being the same at both ends, when the end of the line was reached, the driver would unhitch the horse or horses, and pick up the Whipple trees. These were two wooden pieces that created a solid frame onto which the harness traces were hitched They would then unhitch these whipple trees and attach them to the other end of the car. The back of the car now became the front as they set off in the opposite direction.

Replica of Winnipeg horsecar circa 1880s.
Location: Calgary Heritage Park, Calgary Alberta (Author photograph.)

Horsecar proceeding along Main Street, Winnipeg, Mb
Circa 1882
Winnipeg Transit Photo Archive Collection- Ernest Brown Collection

Passengers in the horsecars sat down on each side of the car facing each other. Approximately 20 to 24 passengers could be seated, with room for that many more standing, when necessary. During the winter months, straw was sometimes spread on the floor of the car to make passengers feet a bit warmer. They also tried using small wood stoves, with limited success. Travel was rather slow since the City decreed that the speed limit of the horsecars could not exceed six miles an hour. With the various stops along the line it is doubtful that this was ever reached, unless, of course, a horse got frightened and a runaway occurred! Just like humans, horses can literally kick over the "traces" or harness when they are startled or upset. In one instance a frightened horse took off with the horsecar trailing behind and was finally stopped when it crashed through a store window and was captured inside! No mention was made of injuries to passengers. On another occasion, a horse developed "blind staggers," which is a disease similar as to what we refer to as insanity. The horse reared, snorted, kicked, bit the conductor, and tipped the car over while trying to climb a lamppost. Again, there was no mention of passenger injuries!

A. W. Austin, founder of Winnipeg Street Railway Company; H.W. Blake Collection

Albert W. Austin, a 23-year-old, whose father was founder of the Dominion Bank in Toronto, arrived in Winnipeg in early 1880. He established and incorporated a company known as the Winnipeg Street Railway Company. Stocks in the company opened for sale on April 28, 1881 and sold out within an hour. Austin led his company for 12 years, until the end of the horsecar era when he was forced to sell out to the newly formed Winnipeg Electric Street Railway Company. Mr. Austin was the force behind the introduction to the first electric streetcar to Winnipeg. The initial run of the service occurred January 27, 1891. Thus Winnipeg became the fifth city in Canada to have electric streetcar service, after Windsor, St. Catherine's, Victoria, and Vancouver. Even Canada's capital city Ottawa didn't have this service for another five weeks, and Toronto and Montreal waited a few weeks more before they could claim electric service. Even New York City didn't have electric cars until 1895. It was no wonder that by 1912 Winnipeg was called, "the Chicago of the North." Chicago had initiated electric streetcars one year earlier, in 1880.

Unfortunately, politics reared its head even in those years. City council was reluctant to allow Austin to operate his four electric streetcars on Main Street, as they were afraid someone might get electrocuted if the trolley pole slipped off the overhead wire. Thus he was made to run them in a mostly uninhabited area. He ran the cars down what is now known as River Avenue, then south alongside the Red River on what later became Osborne Street. The cars then traveled west for a short distance. Ever the entrepreneur, he built an amusement park called River Park at the end of the line. As there were no buses or automobiles in those days, people would ride out to River Park by the thousands on a sunny weekend to ride the merry-go-round and Ferris wheel and enjoy a sociable picnic lunch with family and friends. The streetcar service was such a convenience in this area that many people bought property and built houses in the area, thereby necessitating businesses to spring up to serve the new development.

THE STREETCARS OF WINNIPEG

Winnipeg Open Car #122 – Built in Winnipeg in 1904 and used for summer runs to River Park; Winnipeg Transit Photo Archive Collection

Austin's Early Streetcar #6, built in 1890; Archives of Manitoba Transportation Collection - Streetcar 16 N 7595.

OUR FORGOTTEN HERITAGE

Streetcar #28, built in 1893; Steven Stothers collection photo.

Job descriptions and benefits for drivers improved over time. I'm sure the few horsecar drivers who transferred to the electric cars in the early 1890s saw a vast improvement in their working conditions. They did not have the responsibility of looking after the horses and they could leave the streetcar unattended for a few minutes if they had to (although there were no Starbucks or Tim Horton's in those days to get quick refreshment from). One big improvement was that the front vestibule was enclosed, protecting them from the stormy elements of the weather, and they may have even felt a little heat from a stove in the front of the cars. Around 1908, the strenuous arm-twisting wheels the motormen had to crank to bring the streetcars to a stop were replaced with airbrakes. When compared with earlier conditions, the improvements were significant and must have been very welcome, indeed.

Chapter Two

ELECTRIC CARS IGNITE POLITICAL FEUD

While horsecars were a popular means of transportation in eastern Canada and the United States, as populations became larger and cities spread out, they did not provide a solution to the increasing demand for service. Electricity was still in its infancy in the late 1870s and '80s, and streetcars as we know them today had not yet been invented. There were a couple examples of battery driven streetcars, but they had to stop and recharge the battery every couple of miles. (One can only imagine how long it would take to get somewhere.)

A few experiments were tried employing the "third rail" idea. This method used an enclosed electric wire mounted between the two running rails, but problems developed when water and dirt seeped into the covered wire in the third rail, shorting out the system. Next, they tried transferring the electricity from its overhead wire down to the motors underneath the floor of the car. The trolley pole would be used to conduct the electric current, but it took several attempts before they found a suitable trolley wheel that would ride smoothly and sustain the connection underneath the overhead wire. The next problem was to find a spring that could be mounted on the roof of the car and provide enough tension to hold the pole on the wire. It was a long tedious process to find a workable solution.

The next phase for improvement was to design smaller motors that had more power and more options for speed. The improvements in this sector continued for the next 60 years. Germany had the first operating electric streetcar service in Europe in 1881. In Canada, Windsor commenced service in June 1886. Along with a couple of American cities that same year, these became the first cities in North America to provide electric streetcar service. By 1888, a lot of improvements had been realized and from then on cities lined up to get on board. By 1916, approximately 80 Canadian cities or larger towns had streetcar or interurban service. Interurbans mimicked stretched streetcars and were approximately 50 or 60 feet long. Some looked almost as big as railroad coaches. They were adaptable to the flow of passengers since they could be used as individual cars or, if passenger traffic warranted, as many as three of four at a time could be hitched together. Customer service options increased within the cars as well—some were equipped with washrooms and plush seats, as well as portable tables and curtains--likely quite the novelties for passengers.

OUR FORGOTTEN HERITAGE

Interurban car in front of the ticket office in Selkirk, circa 1920; Mark Perry collection photo.

After 10 years of horsecar service, Winnipeg's population, like other cities, was growing; at close to 30,000 people the horsecars would soon be unable to handle the increased demand. Austin thought his existing horsecar franchise and well-established electric car runs on River and Osborne Avenues would entitle him to run electric cars in Winnipeg proper once city council opened it for tender. Politics entered the picture again. City council said Austin had not officially presented his tender in time to operate electric cars in Winnipeg and James Ross of Montreal and William MacKenzie of Toronto became the successful bidders. Austin took it to the highest court in England but was told the other two men had made a legal bid. Under the ownership of Ross and MacKenzie the new company would be named Winnipeg Electric Street Railway on February 1, 1892. Their first car started to run to the exhibition grounds off Selkirk Avenue on July 26 and they commenced regular service on September 5, 1892.

Opening of Winnipeg Electric Street Railway on Main Street, across from City Hall, September 5, 1892; Archives of Manitoba. Transportation Streetcar 19. ON 152. N 7600.

Austin was persistent in his vision. He continued to operate his horsecars in competition along Main Street and Portage Avenue for another year and a half. Main Street now had four tracks and competition between the two companies brought fares down to 50 tickets for a dollar at one point.

Austin was fighting a losing battle, however, as the electric cars were somewhat larger and much faster—they simply had more capacity to deal with the growing population. In the early part of 1894, the horse barns at Assiniboine and Main caught on fire and more than half of the 80 horses died. This was the beginning of the end of the horsecars and on May 11, 1894 the horsecars made their last run. Ross and MacKenzie bought Austin out, including his four electric streetcars, for $175,000, thereby ending the fierce competition and bringing an end to the horsecar era in Winnipeg.

Chapter Three

FIFTY ELECTRIC STREET CARS BY 1902 "SPARKS" WIDER RANGE OF SERVICE

The Winnipeg Electric Street Railway lost no time in laying more tracks and was soon operating 17 single truck streetcars. Track was established to the west on Portage Avenue to Maryland Street. It made its way to the north up Sherbrooke to Logan Avenue and over to Main Street. It continued north on Main to Inkster Boulevard as well as to Notre Dame Avenue.

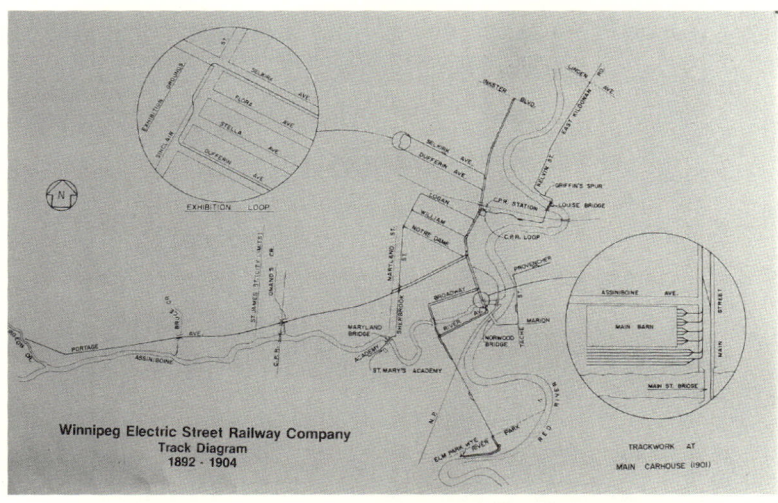

Map of Winnipeg Electric Street Railway Company routes, 1892 – 1904; J. E. Baker, Winnipeg's Electric Transit, p. 22.

Under the commitments of the contract between the City of Winnipeg and the Winnipeg Electric Street Railway Company, streetcar service had to be provided if at least 400 people over five years of age lived along a half-mile of track and within a quarter-mile of each side of the track.

The available transportation service encouraged the city to grow and spread. It gave residents the option of living a reasonable distance from downtown while still finding it convenient to get there (downtown was where most people worked in those days). This was a valuable option since it would still be nearly a decade before the first few automobiles arrived in the city and the arrival of the first buses in 1918 was also years away. Progress continued with the first car barn for the electric cars being built on the south side of Portage between Carlton and Edmonton Streets. In 1893 service was updated through the purchase of sweepers to clear the snow off the tracks in the wintertime.

The new streetcars were capable of doing 30 miles per hour and were 22 feet in length. They could accommodate two dozen passengers seated and an extra dozen people standing at any one time. They also had a coal-fired heater behind the motorman that helped to heat the car in the cold weather and provided comfort for the customers.

OUR FORGOTTEN HERITAGE

Streetcar (left) attached to three trailers and flat band car for musicians – on route to River Park, May 1893; H. W. Blake Collection.

A trailer was often used in summer to take the large crowds to parks and exhibitions. It was slightly smaller than a streetcar with some of the early ones having a roof and open sides and ends. The seven or eight cross-seats each held 4 to 5 passengers and gave riders a good view of the area. A regular streetcar would hook on to a trailer and could tow at least two trailers. The newer cars could pull three trailers when necessary. On special occasions, the streetcars would pull a long flat trailer that transported a musical band that played on the way to the park, and then performed at the park.

Trailers outside Assiniboine Garage; H.W. Blake Collection.

Park Line open car with trailer built in Winnipeg 1901 – '04; Winnipeg Transit Photo Archive Collection.

The streetcars pulling the trailers were built much like the trailers themselves only a bit longer. As more streetcars accumulated, these trailers were phased out gradually and were eliminated by 1914. Ten of them were sold to

OUR FORGOTTEN HERITAGE

Brandon, Manitoba in 1913 when that city began operating its streetcars.

In 1918 Winnipeg took 11 streetcars that had been built in 1912 and made them into "trailers." These had been made slightly longer—about 30 feet and almost the size of the regular streetcars of that time. They were permanently hooked on to a regular car and were used in rush hours on some of the heavy lines such as Portage Avenue, North Main, Osborne, and Selkirk. One motorman and two conductors made up the crew. These were retired in the early 1930s as buses were starting to run on the shorter routes. This change shifted more streetcars to the major lines to handle the increased use of these routes. Transportation by streetcar had peaked by the early '30s; decreasing streetcar ridership was related to the influx of the improved private automobiles.

Chapter Four
A MAJOR STREETCAR BUILDING INDUSTRY DEVELOPS IN WINNIPEG

By 1901 Winnipeg's population exceeded 52,000 people. That year the Winnipeg Electric Street Railway Company had 42 streetcars operating and they carried 500,000 passengers that year. In 1903, after ordering approximately 60 cars from eastern Canada, the company started out on a new venture by building some of their own.

They started by building five open cars as described in the previous chapter, followed in 1904 and 1905 by adding smaller interurban cars #154 and #156. These two cars were destined to run to Headingley, Manitoba, about 12 miles beyond Portage and Main. Track had been installed to Headingley in late 1905, and the "Twins" as these cars were called, commenced service there December 20, 1905. These two cars were 37 feet long and had a 23-foot section that could seat 36 passengers. It also provided a 14-foot baggage compartment.

Headingly interurban car #154 built by the Winnipeg Electric Street Railway Company in 1904; Archives of Manitoba Transportation Collection - Streetcar 18 N7597.

A round trip from Headingly to Higgins and Main took one hour. For the morning and evening rush hour trip when most people were going to or coming from work, the cars ran together. At other times they ran singly to provide a more frequent service in the non-busy times. These cars would stop in the morning at designated spots and pick up farm produce such as cream cans, eggs, and milk and drop them at a depot downtown. In the evening, they would drop off the empty containers at the trackside platforms. If a farmer needed a machinery part they would bring that as well as long as the supplier could deliver it to the loading depot downtown. This was a great help to the Headingley area as there were only a few hundred automobiles in Winnipeg at that time. (The first car had arrived in June 1901.) Headingley had streetcar service for the next 24 years. The last car on the route ran on May 7, 1930.

OUR FORGOTTEN HERITAGE

Although these events were before my driving time, I can remember the various uses of the streetcars and the assorted types of passengers who would on board my car.

Occasionally, an incident transpires that puts a different focus on a humdrum day. One such occurrence happened to me one summer Saturday morning in 1954 as I was operating the #26 North Main streetcar just north of Dufferin and Main. Every Saturday during the summer and fall market gardeners would occupy a vacant lot there with tables and stalls full of garden produce such as potatoes, carrots, beans, corn, and other crops. Some farmers would have eggs, cream, butter, and live chickens for sale. In the fall they would also have live geese and ducks as well. A few would sell fresh baked buns, bread, and sometimes even rhubarb pie. There was always a good crowd of potential buyers in attendance. Plastic bags such as those that supermarkets use now had not been invented yet, so produce bought was put in large paper bags or mid-sized cardboard boxes. However, if a person bought 25 to 50 pounds of produce it was usually placed in large jute potato sacks, which buyers could throw over their shoulders and carry to the streetcar stop. The majority of customers were women. In those days a lot of men worked Saturdays, and if the family had a car the men would have it. As well, in the mid-1950s a lot of mothers stayed home with their kids, and many city mothers didn't drive a car in those days.

As I brought my streetcar to the next stop a large woman boarded my car paid her fare and asked for a transfer. Over her shoulder she carried a large jute sack with two squawking live hens in it. She proceeded about two-thirds of the way down the car and flopped into a double seat. Immediately, the passengers in the seat just in front and behind her moved to other seats, as they didn't want these hens squawking in their ears. There were two dozen passengers on the car so there was lots of room to move around. Most of the people were in their everyday clothes, not going anywhere in particular. However, on the other side of the car, about three seats ahead of the woman with the chickens in a sack was a very well-dressed lady in a smart summer dress; a cream-colored stiff blocked straw hat with a ribbon band and feather completed her outfit.

Inside a Winnipeg Streetcar, circa 1945; Winnipeg Transit Photo Archive Collection LB Foote photo.

All of a sudden the two hens clawed their way out of the sack and started running down the centre aisle toward the front of the car. When the impeccably dressed lady spotted them she gave a loud shriek, thereby scaring the hens. They took flight about seat height to the front of the car and their owner followed close behind. Upon reaching the front of the streetcar, the hens turned around and flew the 40 feet back to the rear of the car. Then they turned around one more time and flew to the front of the car again. By this time they were almost exhausted—domestic fowl can't fly very high or very far. When the owner made a grab for them at the front, one flew back to the rear. On the way back it spotted the well-dressed woman's fancy straw hat and feather and mistook it for a nest, momentarily settling there. Knowing the bird would only be there for a second, the owner raced down the aisle and with both hands pounced on the startled bird squashing the hat down over the woman's eyes. The bird was so traumatized it left a small "memento" of its visit on the woman's crushed hat.

I had stopped the streetcar while all this was going on, as I didn't want the chicken's owner to fall while chasing her birds down the aisle. She had paid good money for them and they were likely that night's supper, so she was very determined! She had no bag or string to control the captured bird so she grabbed it by the legs and held it upside down while she tracked down the other one. By this time a couple of men on the car had pinned the remaining hen against the window until she was able to grab it. She then staggered back to her seat with a upside down squawking chicken in each hand.

I started up the streetcar again and the woman with the crushed hat pushed the buzzer and got off at the next stop, her day ruined, no doubt. The chicken owner hollered, "Let me off when you come to Mountain Avenue!" That was only a few blocks away so I called "Mountain" as the car came to a stop and she came to the front, chickens dangling and hollering, complaining about the status of the flock.

"I need a transfer," she said. I tore one off, but she didn't have a hand to take it.

"Hold it up higher," she yelled, and when I did she ducked down and grabbed it between her teeth, then waddled off the car. As I watched her cross the street to the Mountain bus stop, I pitied the poor Mountain driver—those little puddle jumpers with the low ceilings could only hold about 25 people and there would not be much room for the passengers to get away from the noisy hens.

I carried on with my trip and the two to follow after that, but things seemed rather tame for the rest of my shift. I'm sure there were many stories such as this one on these routes accommodating market or farm stops along the way.

Inside of Streetcar – Circa 1910
Winnipeg Transit Photo Archive Collection L B Foote photo.

In the last few years the Twins were replaced by the 1400 series and occasionally the 1200 series of cars. These were rebuilt cars from older ones with 33-inch wheels for more clearance under the car to operate in deeper snow. They also had a snowblade mounted underneath to clear the track. These cars were mainly used on outlying routes where the snow was more prevalent.

OUR FORGOTTEN HERITAGE

1200 Series streetcar (described below); Winnipeg Transit Photo Archives Collection.

In most cases, the numbered series of the cars indicated their type of structure and capabilities. The streetcars were numbered differently than were the buses—streetcars were given even numbers and the trailers were given odd numbers. This helped to quickly identify structures for maintenance purposes.

There were 29 cars rebuilt in 1924-'25. In 1928 the longest streetcar in Canada, #798, was built here in Winnipeg. It measured 53 feet, 3inches in length and seated 60 passengers. The last to be built here was #796. Built in 1929, the car was approximately the same length as the others and seated about 50 people.

THE STREETCARS OF WINNIPEG

1400 Series streetcar made in 1925; Steven Stothers Collection, Stan Styles photo WEC-1400-1 taken in 1947.

Streetcar #796 was the last streetcar to be built in Winnipeg (1929); Steven Stothers Collection, Stan Styles Photo WEC-796-1 taken in 1947.

OUR FORGOTTEN HERITAGE

**Streetcar #798 in operation on Main Street, built in 1928.
Steven Stothers Collection, Stan Styles photo.**

Over a period of 63 years Winnipeg had approximately 405 streetcars. Of these, 246 were built in Winnipeg. Another 29 were rebuilt into the 1200 and 1400 series. Many of these cars were rebuilt from double-end cars to single-end ones. Changes were always in progress, such as moving from two-man to one-man cars, and replacing 33-inch wheels with 26-inch ones, which allowed for lower and easier boarding.

Between 1931 and 1938, nine streetcars were rebuilt with modern master fronts, created at the Winnipeg Electric Streetcar Company shops in Winnipeg. This addition to the front of a wooden streetcar improved function and streamlined it somewhat; the route number box on the roof of the vestibule was removed and the route number and destination display was relocated to just above the center window. This center window was a lot wider than the regular fronts and was angled out slightly to give the operator a better view of the traffic. Narrower corner windows bordered the center window. Sometimes master fronts were installed if the front of the streetcar had been in a serious accident.

Winnipeg Electric Streetcar Company's Streetcar #386 with master front; built 1909. Last streetcar the author drove Sat. Sept 17, 1955; Steven Stothers Collection Stan Styles Photo WEC-386-1 taken 1947.

When the end of streetcar service came in September 1955 they had about 75 cars left that were operational. A number of the ones still in service at that time were built between 1909 and 1914. The newest cars were #796 and #798, built in 1928-29 and more than 25 years old at that time. During this same period equipment also included 15 snow sweepers and sand and rail grinding cars, as well as wreckers, line cars, flat cars, and a water sprinkler car. There were many aspects to keeping everything serviced and in good running order, especially since 25 of the cars were over 45 years old. This contrasts with current use, as today buses are usually phased out at 18 to 20 years when new models take over.

OUR FORGOTTEN HERITAGE

A rotary plow— built 1904 these massive blades could plow through snow 12 feet deep; Steven Stothers Collection, Stan Styles photo WEC-18-5 taken in 1946.

Streetcar #15, one of 16 snow sweepers used in 64 years of service, built 1920. Steven Stothers Collection, Stan Styles photo WEC-15-3 taken in 1951.

THE STREETCARS OF WINNIPEG

Early line truck to service the 600-volt overhead streetcar trolley pole, circa 1928, Public Service Issue News, Centennial Issue, October 1982; Winnipeg Transit Photo Archive Collection.

This service car travelled to streetcars in need of tools and mechanical repairs; Circa 1930 Winnipeg Transit Photo Archive Collection.

Chapter Five

SERVICE TO SELKIRK 1908- STONEWALL 1914 THE EXPANSION CONTINUES WITH SERVICE TO SELKIRK AND STONEWALL

In 1908 Selkirk, Manitoba joined Winnipeg in streetcar service. After track had been laid from Winnipeg to Selkirk, the first interurban car made its initial run on April 10. Four 60-foot long combination cars—part baggage, part passenger—served the line of approximately 26 miles.

Two of the interurbans serving Stonewall and Selkirk; Winnipeg Transit Photo Archive Collection. Stan Styles photo.

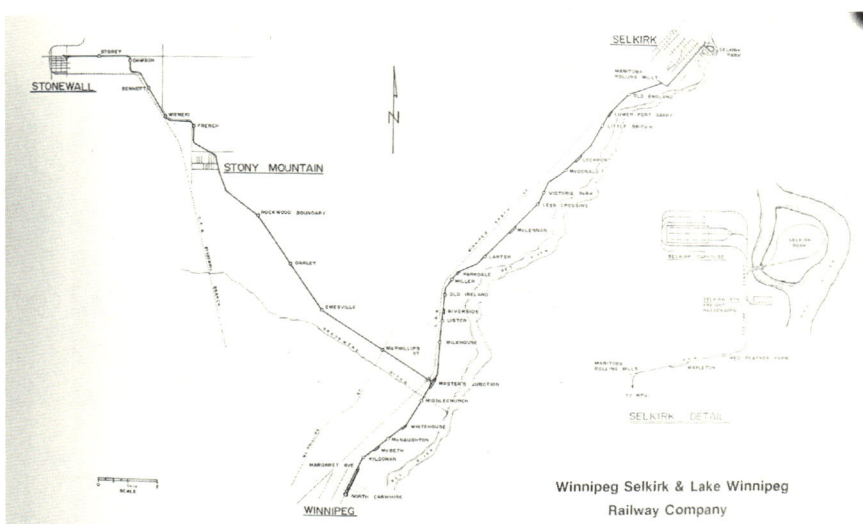

Interurban Map from Winnipeg to Selkirk-Stonewall, 26 miles from end to end; circa 1918 J. E. Baker, Winnipeg's Electric Transit, p. 115.

Three-car combo Interurban on the Lake Winnipeg-Selkirk line; Winnipeg Transit Photo Archive Collection.

There were also two passenger coaches and four trailers about the same length assigned to this line. These could be hooked on to the "combos" or the coaches and could be made into trains when needed. Streetcar service to Selkirk was in operation until the end of August 1937, a period of almost 29 and half years. By that time there were a lot more automobiles on the road—the Interurbans had served their purpose.

In 1909, the Winnipeg Electric Railway Company had 69 miles of track to serve the public. An additional facility, the North Car House was built at this time at Main and Inkster. This provided a place for the Selkirk cars to turn around and made it easy for passengers to transfer from the Selkirk car to a city car to take them downtown. These Selkirk Interurbans also brought produce in to the city from farms in the area, which was a great help to farmers at that time as very few of them had trucks to bring in their goods.

North car house at Luxton and North Main, circa 1920s; Steven Stothers Collection.

In 1914 the town of Stonewall, Manitoba came on track. Regular service began December 14 of that year. The same track north of Winnipeg that the Selkirk cars traveled on was used up to Middlechurch, which was a distance of just a few miles. Then the track took a northwestern direction to Stonewall, a 20-mile journey. The entire route between Winnipeg and Stonewall amounted to 24 miles. The Winnipeg, Selkirk, and Lake Winnipeg Railway Company operated both these lines. The same type of interurban cars described previously was used on both routes. More service was provided on the Selkirk route than Stonewall because there were about 15 small settlements on the route to this larger town.

On special occasions two or more trailer coaches would be hooked up to the "combos" to attend picnics at the Selkirk Park by the river. One could travel to Selkirk and back for only 95 cents and Stonewall was a deal at only 80 cents.

During the busiest time of day cars also left north city limits at the Margaret loop, located just north of the current Kildonan Golf Course, for a Middlechurch return. At that time there were a few small businesses operating and a number of people living a few miles out of the big city—these included market gardeners, small dairy farmers, and those working in the city and living on small acreages that provided them with modest incomes. Just like the city streetcars, Stonewall's 10 "combos"—coaches and trailers—were built in the Winnipeg shops. From the mid-1910s to the late '20s, these cars made between 8 to 11 round trips each day. In 1923, they carried 1,196,000 citizens on this route. These Interurban cars provided a very necessary service to these towns for many years.

But, as in the rest of the country, with many people out of work the depression of the late 1920s and early '30s took its toll on revenue. Transit companies tried to reduce expenses by making the "combos" into one-man cars, thereby eliminating the need for a conductor. That still was not enough. Finally, on September 1, 1937, after more than 29 years, the Selkirk route gave way to buses. Stonewall fought to keep their combo service going as the road to their town was not as good or as traveled as the one to Selkirk, especially in the winter time. Big #18, the rotary snowplow, was used to blow out the track on occasion. But by 1939, with further declining revenue and more automobiles now on the roads, motorman Ray Styles brought the last Interurban out of Stonewall on May 1, 1939, after 24 years of service to the town. That brought an end to suburban streetcar service outside of Winnipeg city limits.

Stonewall car on track in winter making its way through a large volume of snow, circa 1920s; Steven Stothers Collection, Stan Styles photo.

Rotary plow blowing drifting snow banks off Selkirk-Stonewall line, Circa 1920s; Steven Stothers Collection, Stan Styles Collection WEC -18-2.

Streetcar #2 Stonewall car snowbound and out of service, circa1920s; Archives of Manitoba- J. W. Newton Collection.

OUR FORGOTTEN HERITAGE

Stonewall Interurban car, circa 1930s; Winnipeg Transit Photo Archive Collection.

Chapter Six

DOWNTOWN THRIVES WITH T. EATON CO. STORE

On July 15, 1905 the T. Eaton Co. Ltd. store opened at Portage Avenue and Donald Street and a new era was about to begin for the citizens of Winnipeg. The T. Eaton Co. store brought in a new concept of merchandising that had not been seen outside of the city of Toronto. Along with their home delivery in Winnipeg and the mail order business they provided to the rural areas of Manitoba, they became the biggest store in Western Canada. How did customers get to their store to shop? If they lived within 12 blocks they probably walked; if they rode a bicycle they may have travelled a greater distance. But the large majority didn't have these options and there would be no city buses to bring them downtown until 1918, another 13 years away. The answer was streetcars—whether you lived in Headingley, North Main, St. Charles, East Kildonan, or toward Osborne Street—if you were one of the 75,000 residents of Winnipeg you could be picked up and dropped off right in front of the store.

T. Eaton Co. store with the streetcars in front, circa 1910; H. W. Blake Collection.

Within five years the population would increase more than two-fold and the area the streetcars served would also more than double. By 1913, with the need to move more and more people efficiently, streetcars allowed the city spread out to become Canada's third largest city.

The far seeing business man could see the advantage of setting up where customers could easily get to his place of business. (A sort of "build it and they will come" attitude.) The Winnipeg Streetcar Company made sure they could provide service to this area—these complementing services were a good deal for both parties.

In 1913 Winnipeg only had 3,000 automobiles, which wouldn't have made much of a dent in a population that was approaching 170,000 people.

In 1907, a few years after the streetcar tracks had been extended to Headingley, the company built two short spur lines that were like sidetracks to specific destinations. One went to the Kirkfield Park Racetrack and Rifle Range, an area used frequently to train troops during the First World War. The other track ran south to the St. Charles Country Club and was used from spring through to fall.

The St. Charles Country Club was used for many high-class social events, and of course its adjoining golf course was well patronized during the good weather. The company left one of their single truck cars out there for the summer. The caretaker of the club was trained to operate the car. He would operate it on the short track, less than half a mile up to Portage Avenue for members who required a downtown car from there. No fare was charged for this ride and the passengers paid the regular fare on the Portage car. St. Charles Country Club paid a nominal amount for the use of the car for the summer; if it needed repairs it would be replaced with another car.

The spur line to Kirkfield was only used at certain times of the year with cars provided only when necessary and was operated by railway men.

St Charles Country Club Car, 1910; H. W. Blake Collection.

Spur line to Kirkfield Park Racetrack and Rifle Range, 1914; Winnipeg Transit Photo Archive Collection.

One issue that was decided in the early part of the 20th century was that streetcars were finally allowed to operate on Sundays. This had been debated for a few years and had been defeated when voted on by the constituents. However, at the end of June 1906 voters decided by a majority of 60 percent that they wanted streetcar Sunday service; this became a reality on July 8, 1906. The ministers of some of the churches said that being able to have family outings at the park or visit friends in the city who lived some distance away from them would lead people away from the church. However, a majority of the public said they worked six days a week and they were entitled to a day of recreation and relaxation with their families. In some cases though, it made church more available to certain members and even gave them more choices regarding the type of church they wanted to attend. This streetcar transportation was even more appreciated in the cold weather as there were only a few automobiles in the city and they certainly weren't equipped for winter driving.

Another way that streetcars were used on occasion was for funerals. If the funeral was for a very high profile person and the funeral establishment was close to a streetcar track, a number of streetcars would be lined up outside the place where the service was to be held. The front streetcar would be draped appropriately in black while the next car would contain the family; other cars were added as needed for the mourners. In this way, the streetcars had become a personal service for the people of Winnipeg.

Winnipeg streetcar used in funeral procession, 1904; H. W. Blake Collection.

Chapter Seven
THE 1919 STRIKE

Between 1913 and 1919 a number of new streetcar routes were established and other routes already in service were extended farther out into the suburbs.

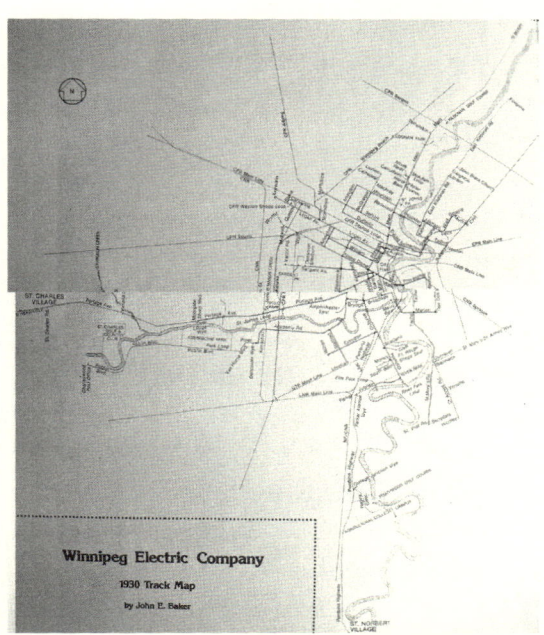

**Winnipeg Electric Streetcar Company 1930 route map;
J. E. Baker, Winnipeg's Electric Transit, p. 108.**

Citizens felt confident buying homes a distance from downtown Winnipeg as they knew streetcar service would be provided to their area shortly, and as a result of this faith in the service Winnipeg continued to expand. The benefit of this service was fully realized in the general strike that hit Winnipeg in May and June of 1919. Streetcar service, with the exception of uncoordinated and sporadic attempts to resume it, was non-existent for the six weeks of the strike. The strike date was May 15 and all unions walked out at that time—the Iron Workers Union was the first to go on strike; other unionized workers walked out in sympathy, including the Winnipeg Street Railway. Part of the problem was the fact a lot of soldiers from the First World War had just returned home a few months earlier and there were too many men and not enough jobs for everyone.

For the first couple of weeks of the strike the unions combined their strengths and no streetcars ran. The City of Winnipeg government formed a Citizens Committee of 1,000 people to try and break the strike. Committee members armed with baseball bats tried to operate a few streetcars—13 in all. Some of the cars had bricks thrown through their windows and eight miles of poles that held up the overhead trolley wire along the track to Selkirk, Manitoba were torn down. June 21, 1919 became known as "Bloody Saturday" when riotous workers attacked streetcar #596 in front of City Hall. They succeeded in tipping it off the rails but it didn't fall over on its side. Next they tried to set it on fire but a fire truck forced its way through the crowd and put it out. Members of the Citizens Committee operated the fire truck as Mayor Charles Gray had fired all the members of the police force and fire department for refusing to go to work. The Mayor read the riot act from City Hall. The Federal Government called in the Royal Canadian Mounted Police and the military complete with a machine gun as the mayor was afraid the rioting crowd was going to overthrow the city government. The RCMP charged the crowd on horseback and in the confusion a man in the street was shot and killed. After this the crowd slowly dispersed and the damaged streetcar was towed back to the barns for repairs.

Streetcar #596 tipped during the general strike, June 1919; Archives of Manitoba Foote Collection 1697 Winnipeg General Strike N2763.

Fire fighters arrive to save streetcar #596 during the general strike, June 1919; Archives of Manitoba LB Foote Collection 1696 Winnipeg General Strike N2762. LB Foote collection. 1697.N2763.

After six weeks the strike was finally called off on June 25. Because of their actions during the strike, a lot of men were not hired back to work on the streetcars. Companies thought they could pay less as many men were anxious to find some form of work. This strike has been a prominently discussed event in Winnipeg's history. (Eighty-six years later it would be remembered via a successful musical play *Strike!*, which was performed at Winnipeg's Rainbow Stage in 2005.

The year 1920 would also prove to be a fateful one for the streetcars. At 10 p.m. on April 7 the streetcar barns at Fort Street and Assiniboine Avenue caught fire. The barn men were able to protect 75 cars from the fire but 20 cars and four sweepers were completely destroyed. The loss of the cars and a good portion of the barns amounted to $400,000 and 100 men were laid off for a few months until the cars could be replaced. Rebuilding the new barn started almost immediately, but getting replacement cars was a different matter. New ones couldn't be promised in time for winter so the purchase of second-hand ones was pursued. After considerable searching, 20 cars were located for sale in Minneapolis/St. Paul. These were wooden cars with bodies much like those of the Winnipeg cars, built in 1908. They were shipped to Winnipeg on flatcars and the workmen there changed the body styles to blend more closely with the Winnipeg cars. New motors, trucks, and controllers were installed and they were all in service by December of that year. The 20 cars were given even numbers, from 800 to 838. They were eventually scrapped in 1949-50, nearly 30 years later.

Streetcar #800—Minneapolis cars built in 1908 arrived in Winnipeg in 1920; Steven Stothers Collection, Stan Styles photo WEC-800-1 taken in 1947.

The 1920 fire highlighted an odd twist of fate in the history of Winnipeg's streetcars. Among those destroyed in that blaze were two small single truck cars, #86 and #106. These cars had been built in 1901-02 and ran on River Avenue. The company tried running bigger cars on the River Avenue route but they were not profitable and so that became the first discontinued streetcar route. The oddity in this is that the River Avenue was the first street that Albert Austin ran the very first electric streetcar to demonstrate its efficiency on January 27, 1891. After the monumental task of chopping down all the trees and clearing the bush, then laying rails and installing poles to hold the overhead trolley wires so that service could be initiated, it all came to an end on the same route 29 years later. On May 19, 1920 streetcar service ended on River Avenue to be replaced some months later by buses.

In the later part of 1919, after the strike, Winnipeg moved away from building their own streetcars and ordered 20 steel cars from Ottawa. They were numbered 702 - 740. Winnipeg followed this up 10 years later building two cars in the style of the Ottawa 700 series.

Ottawa-built 700 series #702, purchased by the City of Winnipeg in 1919, operated until end of service in 1955; Steven Stothers Collection.

Five short, square "Birney" cars were bought in 1921 for the small feeder lines, but they had limited success; all were retired by 1932.

OUR FORGOTTEN HERITAGE

Birney Cars, purchased 1921; Steven Stothers collection, Stan Styles photo WEC-1000-1 taken 1946.

The last wooden car built in Winnipeg was #692, finished just as the First World War started. It was still in service 41 years later when the streetcar era in Winnipeg ended.

Streetcar #692, the last wooden streetcar fully built in Winnipeg in 1914 and operated until end of service in 1955; Steven Stothers collection. Stan Styles Photo WEC 692-1 taken in 1947.

During the Second World War, from 1939 to 1945, a streetcar was painted up to advertise Victory Bonds and war savings stamps. Car #636, a two-man car, was one of the ones used for this purpose. This was the first of a series of enterprising ideas that would incorporate the streetcar into city life and mobilize messages across large areas. Many citizens other than passengers saw the streetcars and their owners capitalized on this, using the initiative several times. After the war they used it to promote special events in the city, such as Winnipeg's 75th birthday party in 1948.

Two-man streetcar #636 with advertising, circa 1930s; Winnipeg Transit Photo Archive Collection.

Chapter Eight
PROFITS AND LOSSES SHAPE WINNIPEG'S STREETCAR CULTURE

One day in February 1942, Canadian soldiers wearing German uniforms took over downtown. They boarded the streetcars and buses and ordered people on or off the vehicles in gruff voices. They marched through stores with their jackboots giving the Nazi salute and ordered customers around. This was an idea dreamed up by the government to let people in Canada, so removed from the war in Europe, to experience similar conditions for just a day. It helped convey the circumstances that Europeans were enduring, and what Canadians could possibly experience in the future.

It was a scheme to promote the sale of war bonds and had a remarkably successful outcome.

During the Second World War there were a lot of women in the work force; the Winnipeg Electric Streetcar Company employed 53 women as streetcar operators who worked regular shifts on the cars according to seniority. As well, there were several women employed in the mechanical sections of the bus and streetcar garages. Three female streetcar operators were still working when streetcar service ended in 1955—two transferred to the telephone switchboard and one established her own business.

A female streetcar operator trains in instruction car #200, circa 1943; Winnipeg Transit Photo Archives Collection.

Women streetcar operators in training, circa 1943; Winnipeg Transit Photo Archive Collection.

OUR FORGOTTEN HERITAGE

In the early 1920s streetcar companies were looking for ways to cut costs as cities across Canada would not grant fares increases except under extreme conditions. At this time, a motorman who drove the car and a conductor who collected fares and controlled the boarding and exiting of people, operated nearly all streetcars. (That is why they were known as two-man cars.) Except for a few on the odd short connecting lines that existed in the outskirts of the city, nearly all the cars in service were two-man cars.

To save themselves paying the wages of conductors, various cities wanted to try one-man cars on all but the very busiest routes. This change would require more controlled access to the streetcar. Entering would have to be at the front of the car only where fares were collected, while exiting could be at either door. The rear door had a steel treadle step. When the operator stopped the car and activated the rear doorstep, departing people who stood on the step would trigger the door to open. If no one else followed the door would close a few seconds after the person walked off the step. Needless to say, the union did not support this idea as such a change meant job loss for the conductors. Although they had opportunities to retrain as motormen, the seniority-based system allowed them to bump the junior motormen out of work. The result was the same: a specific number of men became unemployed.

Actually, many of the motormen and conductors liked working together on the same shift and on the same route. Each one knew the other very well and how they would react under certain circumstances. To clarify, the motorman at the front looks back through his rearview mirror and sees a passenger on the sidewalk starting to run for the streetcar currently situated in the centre of the street. The conductor in the back of the car also notices the determined passenger but every one else has boarded and the doors are clear. He knows the motorman wants to proceed to still get through the green light to stay on schedule. To wait through a red light would result in taking on more passengers that would then put them behind schedule and ultimately they would miss a transfer connection down the track. The domino effect continues…complaints from those passengers who were on the car in time were not transported to their connection in time. So, as the motorman figured he would, the conductor gives him the signal to move (two bells) and the car moves off catching the green light. Downtown streetcars ran every two or three minutes, so passengers did not have long to wait.

In such cases, it was difficult when some of these riders traveled with the same crew several days a week—it was hard to pass them by. Other lines not as restricted by rigid scheduling had more flexibility to wait for those attempting to board.

There were three different runs of the two-man cars and the crews on these ended up having their eight hours of daily work dispersed across all three shifts in the day, anywhere from 6 a.m. to 6:45 p.m. The hours focused on the busiest times of the day including three hours in the morning rush hour, an hour and a half around noon, and three hours in the evening. There were about seven or eight men in total who worked on these three crews. They were all well into their 60s and a few of them nearer 70 years of age. With their high seniority they could have held down straight shifts—consecutive scheduled hours on one-man cars—and could have finished up by 1 p.m., but they preferred to work in a car staffed by two men instead, specifically a car with a motorman and a conductor.

In a two-man car working situation, if one of the men booked off sick or took holidays it usually fell to a "spare man" with limited experience on a two-man car. He would become either the motorman or conductor, whichever position required replacement was. This was quite stressful on both the regular man who might have 30 years on the job and the spare man who may have had only one or two years experience. Each one had to figure out what the other one was going to do in the various situations that arose along the run. If the fill-in was the operator, he might sit and wait for someone waving to the streetcar from the sidewalk. Meanwhile, the conductor with 25 years of experience might have loaded all the passengers, closed the rear door and sounded the two bell "move on" signal to the operator who continued to sit and wait. Or, if the spare man was the conductor, he could have closed the rear door and given the "move on" signal even though a regular passenger who rode several times a week was running for the back door just five or six feet away. Two streetcar men with long time service behind them were synchronized in their thoughts as they drew on their years of experience, whereas the mix of junior-level experience involved a whole new dynamic. The former led to many more happy passengers, and of course repeat business.

Another benefit the two-man car had pertained to managing the impact of the cold winter weather. When streetcars were kept in the car barn they were not allowed to have fires in their stoves. So, to heat a car in a one-man car system, it required the operator to bring his car out onto the track before he could light the stove. In the meantime, he had to keep the car moving at times so he would not get out of sequence on the track. Unlike a traditional bus, you could not just pull around and pass. So at intervals of 10 or 15 seconds, wood kindling was put over the day's supply of newspaper, then one or two minutes later coal was shoveled in to catch the flames from the wood. The balance of technique and timing was important since if the wood burned too long there was not enough heat to light the coal. If you shoveled on too much coal you snuffed the fire out. It was like making a cake; you had to have the exact amount of ingredients stirred in at the right time for the heat to rise. All this of course was taking place while moving down the line and handling passengers. (And in today's world we are told not to text and drive!) It was quite a contrast to today's bus driver who pulls his bus out of a warm garage and turns the heat button to "on," then, in a few minutes he can feel warm air.

On the two-man cars the conductor was an advantage in this regard. Having very few passengers for the first few stops, the conductor could get the fire in the stove under control.

Occasionally, when an unruly passenger had to be escorted off the car, it was nice to have a fellow worker on board for help as there were no phones on the cars in those days. But the two-man car continued to be a challenge and in 1954 Winnipeg ran the last of the two-man cars. When they finished in November of that year one remaining employee went over to the one-man cars while the others retired.

Calgary and Edmonton were the first two cities to bring in one-man cars, in 1917 and 1919, respectively. However, those cities were novices in streetcar experience with only nine or 10 years of service. When Winnipeg switched over to one-man cars on some of the lighter lines in 1924, two-man cars had already been running there for 32 years (since 1892). Hamilton changed over to one-man cars in 1930 and Vancouver lasted another 10 years, changing their system over to one-man cars in 1940.

Chapter Nine

MY FIRST THREE DAYS AS A WINNIPEG STREET CAR OPERATOR

For the first morning of my new job I was directed to go to the Electric Railway Chambers Building at Notre Dame and Portage Avenues at 8 a.m. I boarded the streetcar at Arlington Street and Portage Avenue at about 7:40 and threw in my dime fare (that was the last time I had to put a fare in the box) and rode downtown. When I arrived two other men came in and it turned out they were also from farms, so here we were three farm boys all starting new jobs in the city.

The three of us went to the Assiniboine Garage to meet Chief Instructor Ernie Hales. He introduced us to Instructor Charlie Hays. (That seemed like an appropriate name to three farm boys.) Charlie would instruct us for the first two days. Day one was lectures, learning how to fill out reports, punching and tearing off transfers and learning how to make change with our three-barrel changers. After lunch on the second day Charlie took us up to the North Car House at Luxton and Main. He commandeered a vacant streetcar on a track outside the barn and said, "We are going to climb up on the roof of the streetcar and I'll show you what to do if the trolley pole should break. I shouldn't have to tell you fellows, but you all come from the farm. You would likely fix the problem with some baling wire." Well, the three of us followed Charlie up onto the roof of the streetcar and walked along to portion where the trolley pole was fastened to the roof. Then, as an afterthought, he casually mentioned, "Oh, by the way—don't grab that wire just above your heads—it's got 600 volts flowing through it!"

Once on the ground again Charlie got a motorman and said we were going to make a return trip down Portage Avenue then back to North Car House taking turns being a conductor and taking fares. I should mention here that on the first day we each had to buy $30 worth of tickets and change so we could operate the streetcar with our own money. Fares were then three tickets for 25 cents or 10 cents each, so $30 would normally cover a few trips. We had a two-man car so the motorman was operating the car at the front and Charlie and the three of us were at the rear of the car in the conductor's area. We took turns being the conductor while the other two watched and Charlie stood nearby and gave advice. This is when I got my first lesson how city life differs from farm life.

The three of us each had a company-issued leather bag with a shoulder strap to carry our excess money in. One of the men had hung his bag on a post right beside the conductor's section and the four of us were all standing around in that area of the car. When we got back to the North Car House we discovered that one of the bags of money was missing. How anyone could steal it with four of us standing around that area is a mystery. The following day one of the drivers found the empty leather bag on Selkirk Avenue where the culprit had apparently ditched it.

On the third day the three of us reported to North Car House about 6 a.m. For the next three days we would each be assigned to a two-man car with a regular motorman and conductor. I can still remember the names of my two-man crew after more than 60 years. Staff Morgan was the motorman—to me as a 25-year-old he looked about 70—and Bill Pace, who was a little bit younger, was the conductor. Under Bill Pace's guidance I was to learn the challenges of being a conductor over the next three days.

Sometimes the conductors and motormen weren't too thrilled about training rookies because it slowed them down and they had to abide by the rules more closely. As it turned out, on the morning of the very first day I was with the training crew there had been a three-inch wet April snow the night before, so on my first shift they gave me the switch iron and told me to keep the streetcar steps clear of snow. Later in the day most of the snow had melted so I got to practice conducting for the rest of the three days.

The second week Charlie Hays took us again for a few days and taught us how to operate a streetcar. First in the McAdam field where the streetcars were stored, and then as we got a little more familiar with them we took a couple of trips up North Main to the end of the line at Templeton. We trained with Charlie for about a week. On the third week we operated cars with the regular drivers, gaining experience and receiving useful tips—and, at times, constructive criticism. Then Charlie rode a round trip with us on Portage Avenue picking up passengers. All this training was done on a one-man car, so we also took fares and gave transfers. After the round trip we wrote a couple of exams and signed papers to say we had been taught the various rules and procedures. After that we got the royal handshake and were deemed fully qualified to operate in regular service.

I was given a night run the first week, which was not quite as busy as a day run. But in those days lots of young people took the streetcar to shows, dances, and sporting events because many of them didn't have cars, so certain times of the later evening could be quite busy.

That first evening I took over my streetcar at about 5:20 p.m. It was a straight shift so I wouldn't be finished until after 1 a.m. The operator stepped out of the car, gave me a couple of words of advice on operating it, and then he was gone, finished for the day. I checked the time on the transfers, punched a fresh book of them and positioned the mirrors. I had taken on some passengers in the meantime and the streetcar behind me was giving me the bell to go. But just at that second the light turned red so I had to wait. Turning around and facing the rear of the car I had about 30 passengers. Some of them were reading the paper, a few were talking to their seatmates, and others were just looking out the window thinking about their day. Then I looked at myself in the mirror. I didn't even have a uniform yet. Here I was a farm boy, only three weeks in the city and the only thing I had ever driven before besides a team of horses was a 1928 Model A Ford, a 1947 Ford, and a John Deere tractor. I was in charge of a streetcar worth several thousand dollars, and more than that, I had all these people's lives in my hands and they don't even seem concerned! I looked down and thought to myself - how did I end up here!

Needless to say, I got loaded down going out to Deer Lodge and back again to North Main. After the first round trip I was back on time. I made the rest of my trips without incident and pulled into the North Car House a little after 1 a.m. After closing the windows and pulling down the trolley pole I went inside and signed off my run. My first day was finally over and I felt satisfied with my work.

Chapter Ten
NO LICENSE REQUIRED

In transportation today much more attention is paid to safety and comfort than to most other aspects. In present-day buses, great care is taken to see that the driver's seat is especially padded and that the seatback is shaped to give extra support to prevent strained backs. On the streetcars it was a different set-up. First of all, we had to stand while operating the streetcar through downtown from City Hall to Sherbrooke Street. The Company felt that by standing we would have a quicker reaction to potential problems such as a motorcar suddenly turning in front of us, or a person suddenly darting across the track. This was especially true if it was raining or if there was a strong wind, since most people in such weather walked with their heads down, holding onto their wide-brimmed hats (a definite trend in the '50s).

When we did have an opportunity to sit down our seat was a steel pole (about the size of the ones in today's garden umbrellas) fit into a round socket in the vestibule floor and topped by a hard wooden disc about the size of a dinner plate. While sitting on this "seat" the pole would sway from side to side as the car lurched around curves. The operator had to make sure he had his left hand on the controller handle to keep from falling off when speeds reached 30 miles an hour. The odd thing about it was that you did not hear about many operators with back problems in those days. Of course, in the early days the operators and conductors were in open vestibules, so conditions in the cars did improve over time

A mock up of the inside of a Winnipeg streetcar. From left: stove, schedule holder, black controller with brown operating handle, air brake lever, fare box, and early wheel handbrake (pre-1907). In front is a stool for sitting—notice the size of the seat and that there is no seatback; Manitoba Electrical Museum, author photo.

Streetcar operators had to wear their caps at all times, winter and summer. They also wore a heavy three-piece suit that included a jacket, pants, and vest. In the hot weather operators could work without a vest but were not allowed to take their jackets off. Most men wore white shirts, and a tie while in uniform was mandatory. In the winter they wore a long heavy frieze-type overcoats made with a coarse woolen material. The coat had a high collar to protect the ears, boasted brass buttons, and extended well below the knees. This weighty attire was not replaced until the 1970s, when short, light-weight parka-type jackets became the new winter uniform.

**Long winter frieze coats with brass buttons, circa 1940s;
Public Service News, Centennial Issue, October 1982;
Winnipeg Transit Photo Archive Collection.**

In 1954-55 I was on the spare board for 21 months. We mostly worked six days a week and had no set days off. Hours were set at the discretion of the timekeeper who booked our work. During those 21 months I only had two weeks holiday. During those 21 months I only had two Saturdays off, both specifically asked for—one Saturday for a special day with my parents in the country, and one Saturday was the day I got married! As time went on spare men were given designated days off so they could plan their home lives

When I started in 1954 every operator had to buy a pocket watch and it had to be taken to a jeweller once every year to be cleaned and see that it kept the correct time. The

Company didn't believe in wristwatches saying they didn't keep accurate enough time.

Pocket watch used by author while employed as a Winnipeg streetcar operator; author photo.

My first watch was a 21-jewel Balco. About 20 years later I bought a 17-jewel Waltham pocket watch. I used this watch every day until my retirement and I still have both of them today. The last 30 years on the job I had a wristwatch on my arm but if I wanted to check the time to see if I was on schedule, it would be the pocket watch I consulted. Around the early 1980s when they put the phones in the buses we would get the time signal beep from Ottawa through the CBC at noon each day. I would pull out my pocket watch and were proud to see it was usually within 1 or 2 seconds of the correct time. Now they have cameras in the buses, and some aspect of a GPS.

One of the biggest surprises about the working conditions or requirements was that operators did not need a license to drive the streetcars. In fact, even up to the late 1950s a license was not required to drive an electric trolley bus. The City claimed that because an electric motor propelled it, rather than gas or diesel engine, it did not fall into the category of a motor vehicle. The streetcars were phased out in 1955 and their drivers never needed a license the entire time they were in operation.

The method of non-licensing did provide an option for a few union members who had run afoul of the law operating their own autos. They might have had speeding, alcohol infractions, or careless driving charges applied to their own personal car license. Under a special agreement with the City and the Company, they were allowed to drive their cars if they lived beyond the streetcar service to reach the nearest Company garage. They had to leave their cars there and take transit service to their work location. When their days were finished, they took transit back to where they had left their cars. From there they had to proceed by the shortest route home and could not use their cars for any purpose other than to drive to work. They were not allowed to drive a motorbus at work, but according to seniority, could operate streetcars or trolley buses as they did not require a license. Of course, this ended by the late 1950s.

In the 70s it became mandatory for all bus drivers to qualify for a Class 2 with air brakes. This was one step below the highway truck drivers. But this was the only license we had so if you got more than five demerits either driving a bus or your own car you could be tested again and if you failed you wouldn't be able to drive a bus or your car until you could qualify for a future test. In the meantime your paycheck stopped! Driving 25,000 miles a year in city traffic, especially in winter conditions, and then the thousands of miles put on one's own vehicle highlighted how valuable a driver's license really was. Defensive driving really came into play. As a driver you had to anticipate what the driver ahead of you or beside you was going to do next, even before the driver himself or herself knew. Sometimes you watched your rear view mirrors and if the car following you looked to be too close, you tried to ease the bus up a few extra feet as you approached the stop. It helped sometimes just to have sheer luck, especially if the streets were icy. You would just hope you wouldn't slide sideways into that car that was passing you or maybe one that was parked.

The Company had three different categories for accidents. 1.) chargeable: you were at fault and your safe driving record for that year started over again; 2.) preventable: meaning they thought you could have done something to avoid the accident completely or at least make it much less serious than it was. Again your safety record went back to zero for that year; and 3.) no blame: that was the one you wanted to hear. That usually happened if you were stopped in a bus stop loading or unloading area and a vehicle ran into the back of the bus. It could also take place at a railway crossing. It was mandatory we stop at all railway crossings, even sidings, and motor vehicles would sometimes run into the back of the bus. (Stops at railway crossings are no longer required now unless a train is coming!) Some vehicles came through a stop sign or red light and caused damage. Then again, some cars would speed up, get in front of you and then deliberately stop or drive in your lane at about five miles an hour. A quick temper in this situation was not the best thing to have.

I was fortunate in my 38 years of driving for transit that I accumulated 37 years of no blame accidents. That doesn't mean I never had an accident, but they were all as described above, getting hit at a legal stop. I never hit any vehicle during the 37 years I drove a bus. (For that matter I have had a driver's license since the summer of 1946 and have only been involved in one accident with my car. A guy drove through a residential stop sign at 30 miles an hour and pushed us right across the street into a hedge, causing $7,000 damage to our car.) The one chargeable accident happened at Garry and Portage westbound in the rush hour and I tried to squeeze between the light standard and a two-ton truck and the last three feet of the 40-foot bus scraped the metal hood over the "walk" sign. It didn't pull it off, it just rippled it and it stayed like that for six or seven years, but it was chargeable and I lost my clear accident record for that year.

In a transit career a driver travels many miles. When you assess how many miles a driver covers these same allowances in today's standard seem unimaginable. A driver would average 100 miles a day that would work out to 500 miles a week. Doing the math, this makes me think that in my 38 years I covered around 900,000 miles. There were only two weeks of holidays a year for my first eight years. I then moved up to having three, then five, and finally, after 28 years, I received six weeks holidays a year.

These aren't long distance miles that drivers can accumulate two or three hundred miles a shift. One hundred miles in eight hours comes out to 12-and-a-half miles an hour. In most cases that means pulling in and out of the curb every three or four blocks, fighting your way back out into the fast moving traffic lane on your left, only to repeat the progress again and again until the end of the line. As well, at most stops you are checking fares, giving out transfers, looking at passes, answering questions, and, unlike the Greyhound buses, trying to catch the green traffic light every few blocks. At the same time you have to protect your driving license, for that is your livelihood.

Chapter Eleven
THE WHEELS OF CHANGE

By the 1920s, tracks had been laid in almost every area of the city, but by the end of the decade, as the population neared 220,000, the city was spreading out in all directions and the streetcars were not far behind. The first city buses, four of them in total, started running on Westminster Avenue in 1918—nearly 36 years after the streetcars began service. During the mid 1920s there was a small contingent of buses that appeared on the scene, but these were found on filler routes between the streetcar lines and on a few short outlying routes that had been served by one streetcar. Furthermore, these buses did not come downtown. The advantage the buses did have, of course, was that only one man had to be paid to operate a bus. Up to the mid-1920s all streetcars were operated by two men, as written about earlier.

The first four Winnipeg buses in 1918; Source: Real Estate News, February 14, 1997, JE Baker collection.

As mentioned earlier, two-man cars were costly to staff. Other cities had met this problem by bringing in one-man cars. This extended to Winnipeg in 1924 and was the start of a much larger plan. Barn men, carpenters, and electricians were kept busy bringing streetcars into the barn and changing the car's body style first to suit either one-man or two-man cars. But a year or two later, due to the success of the one-man operations, the majority of the cars were rebuilt to be one-man cars. It cost money to rebuild them it but was much cheaper than buying one-man cars from another source. This was representative of the adaptability that the streetcars had, as this idea would have been almost impossible to accomplish with buses.

A period of many years passed where additional men were not hired. In fact, men were laid off as more one-man cars came into service. This lack of hiring would take place from the late 1920s to shortly before the start of the Second World War. Of course, the depression of the Dirty Thirties, when so many people were out of work, made the situation worse.

Between 1927 and 1932 over 200 streetcars were repainted in their new colors. Streetcars up to that time had their bodies finished in a dark cherry color that matched the wood finishing inside the car. The upright posts dividing the windows as well as the trim above and below the windows were finished in a shade of yellow. This was topped with grey on the roof. All the wooden cars, starting with #350, that were built in 1909 had 10 windows along each side in the passenger section and as a result were called 10-window cars. Wooden cars built before that time usually had nine windows. Earlier ones built around 1900 had fewer—only seven or eight. The bigger steel cars (the #700s) had 13 windows. The new colors also included canary yellow decks, sashes, and letter boards; ivory posts and trim; cherry window sashes; green belt rails with black centres; and large side and end panels in orange and light yellow, painted in a pennant effect. Three cars were painted in this color and tested for several months as to their durability in the weather. The final colors chosen consisted of a light gray roof, maroon deck sash with ivory posts and trim, traction orange body (a pumpkin color,) with a thin black separation line at the belt rail. The trucks, bumpers, fenders, and underbody were painted a glossy black. Though they faded somewhat in color through time and the elements of the weather, they remained in those colors until the end.

THE STREETCARS OF WINNIPEG

The color of streetcars changed from cherry (pictured) to pumpkin orange, circa 1932 ; Steven Stothers Collection.

Streetcar tracks extended towards the outskirts of the city as the need for service increased. Passengers could pick out the right cars for their destinations as the front of the streetcars now had an identifying number that indicated the route of its travels. The sign inside the display box usually contained two white numbers that could be seen from about three-quarters of a block away.

Streetcars had 49 routes in all, numbered from 2 to 99. For example if you saw a car coming with "Portage" indicated at the top of the right-hand front window you could then look at the two numbers in the sign box on the roof. Number 21 told you it went to Deer Lodge, while number 23 meant it traveled past Deer Lodge to Victoria Street. Number 25 would proceed all the way out to St. Charles, while 29 connected at Deer Lodge with the streetcar that went all the way west to Headingley. According to how far down Portage Avenue you lived, you knew by the roof numbers which car or cars would take you to your destination.

Streetcar #646 in front of City Hall on Main Street, May 1948. The number 22 indicates a destination of McAdam and Main; Steven Stothers Collection.

Most of the bigger lines had extension routes and a few of them even had a three-cent zone fare that was paid upon leaving the car. Sometimes two zone fares applied depending on the length of travel. An example of this was on Portage Avenue from Deer Lodge to St. Charles or Headingley. These runs were an extension of the regular line.

Overall, transit fares in 1955 were 10 cents each or three tickets for 25 cents. Children five to 12 years of age traveled for five cents or six tickets for 25 cents. Children under five were free with an adult or older child. In the early 1950s drivers were still selling tickets and making change. Forty dollars was usually required at that time to last a full seven-and-a-half- or eight-hour. The driver was expected to make change for the customers. A leather harness was provided for the driver's change dispenser. It could hold approximately one roll of quarters, dimes, and nickels in the three barrels. As well, pockets were sewn onto the harness to hold tickets. Over time most of the operators just hung the changer on their belt and sewed a couple of divisions in their shirt pockets to hold tickets. As fares increased in the '60s and '70s, operators had to carry more rolls of change and more tickets. During most of that time they carried $130 on a day's run. Unions claimed this was cause for a robbery with possible injuries waiting to happen. Finally, around 1975, they won their case and exact fare was required when riding transit vehicles and operators no longer had to carry change or tickets.

The Company provided drivers with fare slips (which took up the driver's time and were generally a nuisance). If a passenger had no fare or insufficient fare, the operator had to stop and fill out one of these slips. It had to include the date, time, car number, route, operator's badge number, and amount of fare required (10 cents in 1955), and then the passenger signed it. One half was given to the passenger, while the driver turned the other half into the Company. The passenger rode free for that trip but the next time they boarded a car they paid the regular fare plus the fare they should have paid the previous time and had to include the other half of the fare slip they had signed on their last ride. Someone in the office was supposed to watch for these fare slips to see if it matched the one the operator had turned in. One never heard how often these fares were finally paid, but it was a lot of work and resulted in a large amount of lost time for the operator for the sake of 10 cents.

Tickets were three for 25 cents in 1955; Now they are $2.55 each. author photo.

It wasn't uncommon for a supervisor to give you a white card when you picked up your run in the morning. Sometimes they would even approach your bus or streetcar downtown and hand you a card. Quite often the card would say phone such-and-such department and ask for so-and-so. That meant that at the end of your shift you phoned that department and they questioned you about some matter, and, hopefully, you could answer to their satisfaction. On rare occasions it might be to tell you about a compliment one of your passengers had phoned in about you. If the card said "see" that meant right after your shift finished you had to travel down to either the car barns at Assiniboine and Main, or in later years, to Osborne street to be questioned by a particular department.

In the summer of 1954 I received one of these "see" card so after my shift I boarded a St. Mary's bus and got off near the car barn at Assiniboine and Main. They informed me three days earlier I had issued a "short transfer" to a lady who was charged another 10-cent fare (rightly so) by the driver of the connecting bus because her transfer was too late. A short transfer is one that tore off too short and didn't give the customary half hour extra time on it to present to the driver of the bus they needed to connect with. This could easily happen when a number of passengers boarded at the same stop and a handful of transfers were torn off with a quick check of the top one to see that the time is right. Meanwhile, one of the bottom ones might have ridden up a bit on the transfer cutter and be half an hour short. Each driver had his own punch mark in his transfer, so the lady mailed it back to the Company with a request for her dime back as it wasn't her fault the transfer hadn't given her enough time to catch her connecting bus.

They asked me for a dime and said they would send a supervisor out in a cruiser car to deliver it to her. I asked them which street she lived on and I was told that it was just a few streets west of Arlington.

Then I did something you couldn't do now with all the privacy protection in today's world—I said, "Give me her name and house number and I'll deliver the dime myself after my shift tomorrow." Well, to my surprise they went along with that idea, so the next day after my middle shift finished about 1.30 p.m. I rode the streetcar out to her street and walked along until I found the house number. Straightening my tie and my cap I walked up the steps and rang the doorbell. A pleasant looking woman old enough to be my mother came to the door and opened it. In those days it was safe to open the door to a stranger, mind you I was in full transit uniform. I said, "I've come to return your dime you were over charged the other day," holding it out in my hand. She looked flustered and hung her head down and said, "I didn't realize when I wrote that letter the other day that it would cause you all this trouble." I told her the other driver was within his rights charging the extra dime because her transfer was invalid, but it was my fault not hers that it was late.

To smooth out a delicate situation she told me she had just made a pot of tea before I rang and would I come in and join her in a cup? So I went inside and we sat down in her kitchen and had tea and fresh-baked scones. After about 20 minutes, we parted company, each of us with a better opinion of the other person than before we met. Apparently the next day she phoned the transit and said what a nice young man I was! You know something else? To this day I can't remember which of us wound up with the dime!

Chapter Twelve

300 STREET CARS PROVIDE 60 MILLION RIDES

On November 1, 1926, the Hudson's Bay Company store opened at the corner of Memorial Boulevard and Portage Avenue. Two weeks later, tracks were in place on Memorial Boulevard between Portage Avenue and Broadway and streetcar service not only passed in front of "The Bay," as it affectionately became known, but Osborne streetcars could also reach the store via Memorial Boulevard. The Bay, 5 blocks west of Eaton's on Portage Avenue provided the shopping anchor on the west end of Portage and potential businesses tried to open up in that area as shoppers walked the five blocks between the two big stores. This made the land on Portage Avenue between The Bay and Eaton's much more valuable and more riders found it convenient to have so many choices for shopping.

Streetcars were very efficient in moving masses of riders to the majority of these destinations. For example, in 1928, 300 streetcars on nearly 120 miles of streetcar track provided 60 million rides. That's a lot of rides! Winnipeg's population at that time was nearing 200,000 people, so it is quite obvious that the majority of the citizens of Winnipeg rode the cars quite often.

Winnipeg had the fourth highest streetcar track mileage in Canada, which included track extending to Selkirk and the Lake Winnipeg suburban line. Montreal and Toronto had approximately 160 and 155 miles, respectfully, including the many miles of suburban lines there. British Columbia had 242 miles divided among five different transit companies: Victoria, Vancouver, North Vancouver, Saanich, and remote Stave Falls in Northern B.C. Also included in that mileage was the 50-mile suburban track from Vancouver to Chilliwack and the shorter lines to Burnaby and Steveston. Of the 75 to 80 towns and cities in Canada served by streetcars and interurbans, Winnipeg would have been about fourth in individual city track mileage.

By the mid-1930s buses started to make their mark, taking over some of the shorter and outlying stub lines--another new era in transportation was on its way.

Chapter Thirteen
THOSE BEHIND THE SCENES PROVIDE THE MEANS

When the Winnipeg public thinks of transit they probably associate it with the more than 900 drivers of the present-day city buses. Or, seniors might recall the streetcar operators and conductors who provided transportation service during the first half of the last century. But what the public doesn't see is the several hundred employees in the vicinity of the garages whose detailed work keeps the buses on the road so the system can operate. The biggest group in that overall number is made up of the specialized mechanics who service the various components of the buses. These tradespeople have to address the total internal and external systems of each bus, as was done with streetcars in their time.

Another position is the roving repair mechanic. When a driver phones in a problem on the street, this mechanic drives out in his truck and hopes he can correct the difficulty. If not, and if it's not safe to drive the bus, then one of the operators of a transit tow truck will arrive to pull it back to the garage.

There are a number of carpenters and construction men on staff who construct and repair the glass shelters placed at street bus stops so passengers can get out of the weather. As well, they do renovations around the garages as needed. When the streetcars were running a lot of carpenters were needed because more than 200 of Winnipeg's streetcars were built on Osborne Street, just north of their present bus garage. As well, for three decades of the 20th century, carpenters were kept busy changing double-end cars to single-end, as well as altering the bodies of two-man cars to be used as one-man cars. In later years it was these workers who changed the 33-inch wheels over to 26-inch ones. When a streetcar was involved in a major accident it was the carpenters who rebuilt the body as necessary.

Another group is the cleaning staff that put the buses through the "wash rack" after a day's run. In a busy time 40 buses an hour can be processed through the wash rack. In 2014, at the time of this writing, Winnipeg Transit had a fleet of approximately 560 buses. (Of course, there are always a number of buses in for repairs on any given day, or buses that are just not needed at a given time.) Even so, if they had to be all washed in one day it would take over 13 hours.

Let's not forget all these buses have to be filled up with diesel fuel at the end of the day. A full tank is nearly 470 liters of fuel, equivalent to about eight tankfuls for an average larger automobile. Keeping over 500 buses fueled up and ready to roll is an ongoing task.

This synopsis covers most of those who have physical input into keeping the buses on the street. I may have unintentionally missed some additional important roles.

There are numerous other roles that are required for such a successful operation. Every firm needs staff that keeps track of various records to show that the company is operating in an efficient financial way—in the case of transit, to get the most miles for their money. Without administrative support, accountants, office managers, a scheduling department, accident adjudicators, stores suppliers, planners, and advisors, the Company would be oblivious as to their financial gains or losses. These staff members are important cogs that keep the wheels of progress rolling in an efficient manner.

That leaves one more category to cover—the administrators.

In this group we have Supervisors, Instructors, Head of Schedules, a Public Relations Manager, Assistant Superintendents, and a Director of Transit. All are imperative to the smooth running of the operation each day. In any given year there could be 15 to 20 Supervisors. Most of these staff members came up through the ranks as streetcar or bus operators with a good attitude and good record with the Company.

I'm not sure how they operate now with phones in the buses and GPS now in use but in the 1950s to 1970s there would be about half a dozen orange and cream colored cruiser cars driven by Supervisors traveling along the different routes to see that everything was going smoothly. They would stop you and inform you if there was a problem or a potential detour on the line caused by a fire, water main break, accident, parade, or if the bus ahead of you had broken down and you had to hasten to pick up the slack. Sometimes they would just park on the street and watch you drive by checking to see if you were ahead of time or running late. If you were a couple of minutes ahead of time you would likely get a card to phone the office next day. If you had a minor problem with the bus such as low water in the radiator or a jammed fare box (too many dollar bills) they could attend to it or else phone ahead to have a service truck or possibly a new bus to meet you downtown.

A few Supervisors had stationary positions. There was a little glass shack at Fort Street and Portage Avenue that was manned from the beginning of service at around 5:30 a.m. until the last streetcar or bus traveled through Portage and Main about 1:38 a.m. the following morning.

Sometimes in 1954-'55, while on the spare board, I would operate that last streetcar. We would come down from Templeton North Main and arrive at Portage and Main at 1:35 a.m. You had to wait to see that the buses from St. Mary's, Osborne, and Corydon had all arrived from the south because there were usually a few workers who wanted to travel west out Portage Avenue. Danny McClure was the Night Supervisor at Portage and Main and he lived on Duffield Street on the west side of Deer Lodge Hospital. At 1:38 a.m., with all the connecting buses in, Danny would lock up the shack and walk over to my streetcar. "You can go sit down," he would tell me, then he would grab the controls, close the door and away we went. At that time of the morning we might have had only eight or 10 passengers on board and may have picked up three or four stragglers out to St. James, so Danny gave us a swift ride out there. When we got to Duffield Street, which was not a stop, Danny would throw the door open when the car stopped, turn to me and say, " It's all yours, kid. Take her away," and he would jump out and walk up his street. Well I only had one block to go to the turning loop, change my signs and head back to the North Car House arriving about 2:40 a.m. and wait a few minutes for the night workers bus. It was the same end to the shift each night that I worked that run. Danny was always a guy who got things done. I always knew how my evening would wind down on those nights.

In the 1960s after Polo Park opened up Danny was Supervisor in that area. He ran a one-man show and solved nearly all the transportation problems in his territory just by commandeering buses on a slack line and sending them to a different destination. Meanwhile, he would turn the delayed bus around and get it back on time by using a shorter route. One time he told me to punch out two minutes sharp when I got to the Ness loop because the bus ahead of me out there was stalled. Two days later I had to go to the office and they wanted to know why I had punched two minutes sharp. When I told them I was just following Danny's orders because the bus ahead was stalled, they gave a look that said, "We might have known."

The odd time, Supervisors liked to use their power. One noon hour I was running Portage Express west bound at Garry and Portage. This was after we had the phones in the buses. I loaded my passengers, closed the door, and looked at my pocket watch. It was 20 seconds before 12:18, my time for leaving Garry and Portage but the light was still green. If I waited the rest of that green light and also sat through the red light I would have been 45 seconds late leaving Garry so I drove out and pulled into Eaton's stop at Donald Street. I had just started to load when the bus phone rang. When I answered it was the Portage and Main Supervisor phoning to ask me what time I had? My time was correct so he said why did you leave Garry 20 seconds sharp? I told him if I had waited through the green light and then waited on the red I would have left Garry 45 seconds late and you could soon use up an extra 20 seconds loading at Eaton's.

I have yet to mention one very important position, and that would be the Chief Time Keeper. Next to the Lord above, he had more daily control over you than anyone else in the system. As a spare man with no run of your own, he was the one who booked your work every day, even deciding which days you should have off. Ernie Chillwell appeared as quite a stern man, but in my opinion he was always fair. Sometimes I wasn't happy with the work assigned to me, but it was all done according to seniority so I accepted it as part of the job. He did have a soft spot tucked away under that grim look he sometimes wore when you asked him a question he didn't think needed to be answered. Later, when I worked out of Assiniboine Garage, Larry Anderson and Ed Laforme (who later became Superintendent) were Time Keepers at that location.

Instructors were another important part of the system. They were the ones you first became involved with and the ones who gave you your first impression of the job. I still can remember some of the early instructors I worked with, in addition to Charlie Hays, were Bert Wildsmith, Dave Hainsworth, and Ed Schmidt, but there were many others over the years.

That brings us down to the top two positions— Superintendent of Transit and Assistant Superintendent. Mr. Jones was the Superintendent when I started. He was a short, rather pudgy Welshman very seldom seen out on the street during working hours. He always appeared in a suit and tie and he had a soft voice. My one experience with him didn't impress me. After 17 months on the job I had not had any holidays yet as the best period available to me, with my low seniority, was the first two weeks in November. I was getting married the last week in August and I asked him if it would be possible to change one week of my November holidays to the end of August. Neither my wife or I wanted to take a short honeymoon in November nor did I want to get married and go to work the next day. It sounded a reasonable request to me, but when the idea was presented to Mr. Jones he said, "I can't do that for you. If I did, a lot of other men would want the same thing!" I thought the majority of operators are already married and how many single men would get married just to get a few days holiday in August! However, down the road someone else took up my cause and we did get our holiday in August when we got married.

OUR FORGOTTEN HERITAGE

Another fellow that left a better impression on me was Ned Jordan the Assistant Superintendent. The two men were as different as black and white. Ned was a tall man and the wide-brimmed Stetson hat that he always wore made him look taller. On his feet he wore high-top leather cowboy boots. In the cooler weather he wore a leather jacket and just ordinary work pants. Sometimes you might see him with a cigar. He was a bit of a loner—not often seen driving or sitting with anyone. But he certainly knew what was going on in the system. Every day you would see him driving in a cruiser on the street watching to see if everything was operating as planned. If you had trouble with your streetcar or bus he would come over to see what the problem was. I'll always remember one rainy dark October night in 1956 I was driving a 700 "Brill" bus at the end of Talbot Avenue. The road was ripped up for new pavement and the detour was quite muddy and slippery in the rain. About 10 o'clock at night I slipped off the detour partly into the ditch and tried, unsuccessfully, to get out; I just dug a hole with the rear duals. So I picked my way through the mud to a service station that was still open and phoned the Company to send the big tow truck. Then I walked back to my bus and waited for it to arrive. After a while two pairs of headlights approached me—one was the tow truck and the other was Ned Jordan in his cruiser. The tow truck had to turn around and back up a stretch to get to me. Ned in his Stetson and cowboy boots stood out in the rain guiding the tow truck back. When the truck backed to with in four feet of the bus, Ned got down on his knees in the mud and had the tow chain hooked under the bus bumper by the time the truck driver got out of the truck. Then he stood on the steps of the bus and told me how much power to apply to help the tow truck get me out. Once I was out and unhooked he came back to me stuck his head in the doorway of my bus, and said, "Take it back to the garage son and go home. You've had enough for one day." I never forgot that and always had great respect for him after that.

Transit did have a few "perks" for members who had good safety records. Every five years with no chargeable or preventable accidents entitled you to one of the following: a travel clock, a pen and pencil set, a flashlight, a Transit belt, tote bag, or sleeveless sweater, each one with the Winnipeg Transit Logo on them. I collected all six of them during my career. They also had a Drivers of the Month Club—each month, two drivers who had received recommendations from passengers for that month were selected out of the over 900. At the end of the calendar year the 24 operators and spouses or partners were invited to a dinner after which one of those 24 would be selected Driver of the Year. There was no monetary value but you received a framed picture of yourself with the above title inscribed on it. I was fortunate to have received that honor in 1988 after twice being Driver of the Month.

After 22 years of retirement I still have many good memories about Winnipeg Transit. Now if we could just get streetcar #356 back on track, that would be the best memory of all.

In today's world, transit operators probably receive a fair wage for their work efforts. In 1954 we almost went on strike when they tried to reduce our wages by a dime or so an hour, but before a strike took place we actually received a 10-cent raise to bring us up to around two dollars an hour. It's more than 10 times that now.

Whether the streetcar conductors and operators of yesterday, or the bus drivers of today, these people were or are paid to transport passengers to their destination according to routes and schedules, using safe driving practices in accordance with the state of the route and weather conditions. However, the majority of operators do more than that during their daily operations. For example, at 8 a.m. on a weekday morning a downtown Portage Express bus pulls into the eastbound stop at Portage and Arlington. He loads the passengers standing at the stop, closes the door, and checks his watch—he is running about one minute late. The light is still green. He is about to move forward when to his left he notices the south-bound Arlington bus has just pulled in on the north side of Portage Avenue and passengers are waiting for the light to turn red so they can catch that Express bus and get to work on time.

Quickly checking his rear view mirror, the Express driver doesn't see any bus behind him, so they could be waiting five minutes for the next downtown bus. Just like a referee at a football or hockey game, or a home plate umpire in baseball, the driver has to make an instant decision, and there is no instant replay in this case. If he waits for the Arlington passengers he will leave even later, but he will get a few smiles from those running across Portage Avenue who catch him. On the negative side, will he still catch that southbound Sherbrook bus at Maryland and Portage that takes people to the offices on Broadway? It's a win/lose situation, and once that snap decision is made there is no turning back. In this situation he is trying to go above and beyond what he is getting paid for. I'm not saying he should be financially tipped, but at least be recognized for his efforts.

By the way, during my 38 years working for transit I got two twenty-five cent tips, both from drunks! Occasionally, when the fare could have been 60 cents, a person wanting to do something nice would throw 3 quarters in the fare box and say there's a tip for you not realizing we had no access to the fare box. Ah, such is life in the fast lane!

Reliability, dependability, capability. Those three words best exemplify the qualifications transit management have always looked for in new and even long-term employees. They must be reliable in that they will carry out their work assignments according to instructions in a safe manner. They must be dependable in that management can count on them to handle unforeseen situations that came up during their shifts in a safe and courteous manner, causing the least amount of confusion and frustration.

(Actually, bus drivers are really working on their own and are charged with the responsibility of the safe care of several hundred passengers in a days' work. Sometimes decisions have to be made immediately and can't wait until for consultation with transit authorities, although they should always be reported at the earliest opportunity.) They must be capable, mentally and physically, of handling the duties assigned to you in a safe and acceptable manner. It also is a bonus and will make your workload a little easier if you don't have a short temper!

The Company depends on transit workers to show up for work on time. Over the years hundreds of streetcars and buses were booked out every day because the public expected to be transported to their destinations according to the schedules. In the garage there could be three or four spare men on call if a regular slept in or missed taking over their run on the street. But if 10 drivers missed, then bus routes would be missing some buses and people would be left standing on the street. With day runs starting anytime from 5 a.m. to around 6:45 a.m. you can see that it would be easy to miss your run if you weren't an early riser. If you missed your run by more than a minute you lost your whole day's pay. You did have the option of hanging around on the chance a piece of work came up later in the morning after all the reporting drivers had received their work. If you accepted that work you received pay only for the hours in that piece. If you didn't take it you went home with no payment for the day. Some drivers were forced to work nights because they couldn't wake up that early in the morning.

I worked days for 37 of my 38 years and only missed my run three times. Two of those times I was at the garage 10 minutes after my run began and I got some hours of work later in the day. The third time I really slept in by a couple of hours and didn't get any pay that day.

Chapter Fourteen

FIRST REGULAR TROLLEY BUSES IN CANADA

In time, the electric trolley bus appeared on the scene and Winnipeg became the first Canadian city to put them into regular service. The first six Mack trolley buses commenced service on Sargent Avenue on November 21, 1938. The City of Toronto experimented with a handful of trolley buses a few years prior, but did not use them regularly and eventually stopped for some time. It took several years before Toronto began to operate them on a permanent basis. Winnipeg had 22 Mack trolley buses in total, which were all retired in 1960.

Four of the original six Mack trolley buses in 1938; Archives of Manitoba LB Foote Collection N2647.

It was not easy to find replacements for them as many trolley bus builders had either closed down or wanted an order of 150 units to make it a worthwhile production run. In 1945, Winnipeg bought eight Pullman trolleys from the US. In 1956 the City purchased 18 second-hand Pullmans (eight years old), from Providence Rhode Island, and 10 five-year-old ACF Brills T46s from Flint Michigan. During the winter of 1956-'57 these 28 trolley buses were given a considerable overhaul in the Winnipeg garages. The last rebuilt bus went into service in mid-March 1957. A number of new Brills had been bought after the war before a lot of the trolley builders had closed down. In 1957, Winnipeg had a total of 162 trolley buses on hand before scrapping the first Macks in 1960. One Motor Coach Industries trolley bus was built in Winnipeg—#1532. The Company had hoped to build more, but it was February 1942 and because of the war they could not get the materials to build more. Up until 1946, trolley buses took over from streetcars on Sargent Avenue and on the Logan Notre Dame route. Then in the later 1940s and earlier 1950s they took over the other remaining streetcar lines. By December 1954, Portage-North Main was the only remaining streetcar route. However even trolley buses had their "time" in transporting the riding public and by the fall of 1970, again as in streetcars, North Main was the last trolley line to go. This time North Main was hooked up with Corydon Avenue up to Kenaston Boulevard, whereas previously with the streetcars, the route had been running down Portage Avenue to Deer Lodge.

Photo of the first Mack trolley bus, 1938; J. E. Baker Collection.

Second last trolley bus, October 30, 1970; J. E. Baker photo.

So, almost 32 years after the first trolley bus ran down Sargent Avenue, the last one to pulled into the trolley garage at North Main and Carruthers, on the dark evening of October 30, 1970. At 9:05 p.m. that same evening, the operator at the Mill Street Substation pulled the switch to cut off the final power for electrical transportation. This was after 63 years of supplying electrical power from that location, beginning in 1907. As of that moment diesel buses would supply all future public transportation service in Winnipeg and another transportation era had ended.

Winnipeg had a total of 162 trolley buses over those 32 years. Like the streetcars, most of the trolley buses were scrapped at the end of service, however, 15 were sold to Edmonton for parts, five went to BC Hydro, two to Western Flyer, and ten to Mexico City.

OUR FORGOTTEN HERITAGE

The electric power that had propelled the streetcars and trolley buses for 78 years was switched off for last time on October, 30, 1970; J. E. Baker photo.

In the late 1940s the streetcars were still providing committed service on some of the heavy lines. In 1946, with a little help from the two trolley bus lines, Sargent and Logan Notre Dame, the Winnipeg Electric Streetcar Company carried 106 million passengers. By comparison, in 2004 Winnipeg Transit carried 38 million riders using at least 500 buses, drawing from a population that is at least a third larger than it was in 1946. The streetcars accomplished their task with less than half the number of streetcars when compared to approximately 500 buses today.

Trolley buses—the good the bad and the ugly

The good part about them: they were faster, especially from a standing start, than the gas and, later, diesel buses, and certainly than the streetcars. They were much warmer with their electric heaters than the motorbuses of that era, and decidedly warmer than the streetcars. They always seemed to put bald rear dual tires on the rear axel, so on a slippery street your wheels spun on acceleration and made braking more difficult in the snow or icy streets. One drawback that would often happen especially in the evening rush hour, more so in the winter when house lights were on and residential appliances were more in use, would be that trolley buses at the far end of the line would find it hard to obtain enough power to move the bus. The more you couldn't get enough power to move, the harder you tramped on the power pedal. Of course this didn't solve anything. A number of drivers would have to take their foot off the pedal and then some of the buses would start to move. Once a bus got moving for a block or so, it would gradually pick up speed, and as it started returning to downtown it would pick up more power. The older Macks and Pullmans experienced more problems with this than the Brills. It only seemed to affect the buses in the evening rush hour—the rest of the day was okay. Today with all of our modernization of electricity this would of course likely never occur.

OUR FORGOTTEN HERITAGE

Electric trolley bus at Portage and Kennedy, late 1960s; Steven Stothers Collection.

One of the bad problems operating a trolley bus was the restriction to routes you could travel. Naturally, you would have to stay close to the overhead wires that supplied the electric power for the bus, but what happened if you came across a water break on the street, a fire, or another serious situation where the street is blocked? You could only move the bus 12 feet to either side of the overhead wires and if that doesn't give you enough room to get around the obstacle then you were stuck there until the path was cleared through the wreckage or the tow truck came to pull you around it. Another difficulty experienced in the wintertime in particular on the main downtown streets was that the snow would pile up three or four feet away from the curb. This caused obstructions on the route because cars now sat in spots that were normally clear. As long as motorists could see the head of the parking meter sticking up through the snow bank they would climb over it to put their money in and leave their vehicle even though it might be five feet out from the actual curb. Together with the snow, the edge of the vehicle was now about 12 feet out from the curb. Maneuvering through this could become very difficult. Since you could only be 12 feet away from the overhead wires to maintain power you can see the challenge this created.

For example, on your route you are restricted by a delivery truck that has stopped to make a drop off and the driver double parked to run in with his package. You have two choices: wait until the driver comes back—but how long will that be? Or, take a gamble that you can make it around the truck. If the left lane beside you was clear of traffic, you would pull out and go! The trick was to give it enough power in the second or two before your poles come off to coast around him and get back in under the wires again in front of the truck. In the meantime hopefully, your swinging trolley poles won't have hit a street pole or sign and broken in two. If they survived you would then have to get out in the cold and release the trolley ropes and guide your poles back on the wires again. In the meantime you lost four or five minutes from your schedule. Quite often the most frustrating part, out there in the cold putting the poles back on, is that the truck driver would come out of the store and drive off oblivious to the commotion he has caused.

Now here is the ugly part. You are driving down Portage Avenue on a night run and it's thundering and pouring rain. There are quite a few overhead switches on the wires above the bus. You have to make sure your trolley pole wheels that contact the wires just coast through the switch with its power "off" to go straight. If you want to turn, you need power "on" as they go through the switch to activate it. If you travel through the switch too fast your poles will come off whether you want to turn or go straight. When that happens everything goes dark! You get out in your shirt and pants run to the back of the bus and, looking up in the pouring rain in the semi-darkness, try to encourage the two poles to make contact with the wire again. Once that happens, the bus lights up again. Now you are back in your driver's seat again, soaked to the skin but you still have four hours to go to finish your shift. If this happens in the winter time you don't get wet but it can get pretty cold hanging on to a couple of frozen ropes at - 30 C.

Sometimes the streetcar trolley poles came off of the overhead voltage wires, but there was only one of them and drivers could pull down the back window, reach out, and put the pole back on without being completely outside in the inclement weather. That was a bonus!

Trolley buses were in service for the first 17 years of my time with transit. During that period I operated all the trolley routes at some time or other, but as I gained more seniority I tried to pick a diesel run instead of trolleys for the reasons stated above, unless I would get a much earlier finish than what I could have with a diesel bus. Avoiding the trollies lessened the obstacles in my day.

Chapter Fifteen
WINNIPEG STREETCARS REACH THE END OF THE LINE

By the early 1950s Montreal, Vancouver, Ottawa, Winnipeg, and Toronto were the only remaining cities to still run streetcars in Canada. Five suburban lines, one in Vancouver and four in Ontario and Quebec, were also still in operation. They were all gone by the end of the decade with the exception of some remaining in Toronto, which in 2014 still ran a portion of their transportation system with new streetcars; there is also an area that operates a few of the 1940 PCC cars. In most of these cities the streetcars were living on borrowed time. With the exception of two cars, Winnipeg's newest cars were 27 years old in 1955 and a number of the wooden cars were 18 years older than that. When the last few days of service took place in September 1955, they had about 75 streetcars that were still operating. During the war, the public was quite restricted as to automobile trips. Even a trip to work was restricted, as gas was rationed at that time. There were no new automobiles manufactured the last three years of the war from late 1942 to the end of 1945. By 1947, new car manufacturing was in full swing and nearly every male adult clamored for a new car, or at least a better secondhand one. The result was that the public transit system that had stood by its citizens for over 65 years took a huge hit from reduced ridership. It was happening all over North America, and it was just a matter of time before the streetcars reached the end of the line.

As mentioned previously, that time came in the fall of 1955. The city was down to one final streetcar line, Portage North Main. The last revenue streetcar, #734, operated by Leonard Kolley, left the Portage Avenue Deer Lodge loop around 2 a.m. Sunday, . It arrived at North Car House about 2:45 a.m., thereby ending nearly 73 years of streetcar service and revenue. Later that Sunday three cars and a sweeper deadheaded out to the St. James loop off Portage Avenue across from the old racetrack (now Polo Park). They sat there overnight and early the next afternoon, September 19, they headed east down the track toward downtown. When they reached The Bay, police blocked off all the traffic as the cars proceeded slowly to Portage and Main. The first car, #374, a wooden car built in Winnipeg in 1909, was operated by Francis Daly, one of three remaining female streetcar operators. Next was a McGuire Cummings with double truck sweeper #10, built in 1918 and used to clear the track of snow in the winter. Third in the line was the newest car in the system, #796, the steel car built here in Winnipeg in 1929 and referred to earlier in this book. The last streetcar and the final one to go through Portage and Main was #798, a steel car also built in Winnipeg in 1928, was operated by Superintendent Bill Jones. (Remember that #798 had the distinction of being the longest streetcar in Canada at 53 feet 3 inches.) The three streetcars were full of city and transit dignitaries. The procession made a stop just before Portage and Main. Mr. Carter, the Chairman of the Greater Winnipeg Transit Commission, gave a brief speech, then Mayor George Sharpe and the 12 reeves of the surrounding area went through the motions of lifting a section of the west-bound streetcar track to symbolize this was the end of service.

Then #374, with its painted-on tears on the front windows, lurched forward. A quiet hush fell over the assembled gathering as they watched the four cars go around the corner of Portage and Main and head north out of view. Some of the several thousand people who witnessed these proceedings shed a few real tears for the great service the streetcars had given over their 73 years.

They arrived at the north car barns soon after and were stored there for a short time before being scrapped.

In the year 2014 it will be almost 60 years since the last streetcar operated in Winnipeg. We are now headed into the third generation of citizens who have never experienced this part of our history. By another seven years you won't even be able to talk to a former Transit employee who operated one.

Yes, it feels like out of sight--out of mind!

Gathering and ceremony to acknowledge the end of the streetcar era in Winnipeg, September 19, 1955; Archives of Manitoba Transportation Streetcar 4. N 7585.

The last run of streetcars at Portage and Main, Winnipeg, September 19, 1955; Archives of Manitoba. Transportation Streetcar 1. N7583.

OUR FORGOTTEN HERITAGE

Streetcar #374 on the last day of service, September 19, 1955. John Baker Collection

Chapter Sixteen

JOHN BAKER'S BOOK A WEALTH OF INFORMATION

The late Mr. John Baker, author of the book *Winnipeg's Electric Transit: The Story of Winnipeg's Streetcars and Trolley Buses*, spent 20 years doing research prior to writing his book. The book contains 192 pages of information and provides 300 pictures of mostly streetcars, but also a few of trolley buses of various types and models that provided the citizens of Winnipeg with electric transportation.

To my knowledge, no other books have come on the market about Winnipeg streetcars since Baker's book was published in 1982. This book is long out of print and no other publication on this subject appears to be displayed in the bookstores. Regarding the final day that the streetcars passed through Portage and Main—and referring to Canada's, Manitoba's, and Winnipeg's Centennial celebrations in 1967, 1970, and 1973, respectfully—Mr. Baker stated the following:

"The recent Canadian, Manitoba, and Winnipeg Centennial celebrations have emphasized the fact that there is now a whole generation which remembers nothing of the big orange cars, nothing of their size, power or atmosphere. It is for this generation, and for those preceding who do remember, that these chapters have been written." (*Winnipeg's Electric Transit: The Story of Winnipeg's Streetcars and Trolley Buses*, John E. Baker, 1982, p.105.)

The author thought that 27 years after the streetcars' final run, it was important to make this information available to keep the local public in touch with their history. Now, in 2014, another 32 years have passed since he published that statement and almost 60 years have passed since that historic day. It is even more important that the younger generations have the opportunity to have some knowledge of our city's early beginnings and progressive growth.

For those residents who were born here after 1955, there would have been no chance of seeing a Winnipeg streetcar operate. Even for the smaller number born between 1950 and 1955, it is doubtful if many at 3 to 5 years old would remember any of the details if they by chance rode on the cars with their parents. This would also apply to adults who moved to Winnipeg to live after 1955.

Those under 60 would likely make up the largest majority of the population.

The main purpose of providing these facts here is twofold: First, to inform the younger, larger percentage of the population about the immense contribution that the streetcars made toward the growth of the city by providing transportation for almost three-quarters of a century. Second, to bring back some of the memories to the older residents of the city who rode those same cars in their younger days.

Some 43 years back, another transit enthusiast, Herbert W. Blake, compiled two books about streetcars and Interurbans, both published in 1971. Even after an absence of streetcars in Winnipeg for only 16 years, the author felt more information and pictures of the cars should be made available to the public, as even then there would be

OUR FORGOTTEN HERITAGE

20-year-olds who were not familiar with their existence. Blake's first book, *The Era of Streetcars in Winnipeg 1881 --1955* contained 80 pages and 122 pictures. The companion book, *The Era of Interurbans in Winnipeg 1902—1939,* depicted the larger suburban cars that ran to Selkirk and Stonewall Manitoba, distances of approximately 25 and 20 miles. The smaller suburban cars to Headingley were also included. This book of 36 pages contained 51 pictures. While not nearly as detailed as the Baker edition, like this publication, its purpose was to at least provide limited historical information of the streetcars and interurbans and give some background about them and their relation to the expansion of a small city of 8,000 to nearly half a million people by the late 1950s. Unfortunately, these two books are also out of print and like Baker's book the information they contained is not available in the bookstores anymore.

Chapter Seventeen

CAR #356—HAS OUR STREET CAR HERITAGE COME TO THIS?

In 2014 the question might be asked, "What happened to those 400 streetcars that passed through Portage and Main from 1892 to 1955?" There were only about 75 streetcars available for work in their last year of service. By the end of 1955, nearly all of the cars had been sold for scrap. The seats, wheels, controllers, and most metal parts were removed and the bodies were sold for a hundred dollars. The ones they didn't sell were crushed and disposed of. A few were bought for miscellaneous uses such as storing grain, chicken coops, and occasionally even a summer cabin at the lake. But after a few years, ideas changed and when they had served their original purpose, they were often taken apart and used for firewood.

THE STREETCARS OF WINNIPEG

Streetcar #692, the last wooden streetcar made in Winnipeg at the Fort Rouge shops, 1914; Steven Stothers collection, Stan Styles photo.

The author is reunited with #692 in 2012, 57 years after he last drove it—#692 was sold off in 1955 for $100 and is now a beach dwelling near Lake Winnipeg; Author photo.

Out of those 400 cars, only one car has been salvaged. It was a wooden car built in 1909 in Winnipeg's Fort Rouge shops. The streetcar in question is #356. It operated on the streets of Winnipeg from 1909 until the abandonment of service in 1955, a total of 46 years. During that time it was remodeled a few times from a two-man car to a one-man car and from a high-floor car with 33-inch wheels to 26-inch ones for easier boarding. In the fall of 1955, it was one of the few bought, and after being stripped of it's salvageable parts, it was trucked out on a flatbed to the outskirts of Winnipeg at Springfield and Panet Road.

The car was repurchased around 1980 and moved back to the city. After sitting outside for 25 years it was in rough shape. Finding indoor storage in Winnipeg would prove quite a problem, and it changed owners a few times, from the Old Market Square Association to Mid West Rail and Heritage Winnipeg. By 1989, after some time in storage at Winnipeg Hydro's Mill Street substation it was moved to the transit garage on Osborne Street. Eventually, in 1996, it was moved undercover to the Via Rail station in Winnipeg's Railway Museum. It has resided there for the past 18 years and is in a sad state of repair. It needs new trucks, a controller, motors, all metal parts, a new electrical system, seats, as well as new paint and upholstery. It would surely need several hundred thousand dollars to make it ready to operate again.

Streetcar #356 being moved to its present location at the Railway Museum, 1996; John Baker photo.

Chapter Eighteen

SIX CANADIAN CITIES HAVE HERITAGE STREETCARS

As mentioned previously, Toronto is the only Canadian city that operates streetcars as part of their <u>daily</u> service to the public. They have a number of new streetcars including some articulated ones. These complement the subway system and the regular bus service. They also have a few older PCC cars from the 1940s running in limited service along the waterfront as a tourist attraction.

If you want to see streetcars operating in Canada, at least in the summer time, there are six heritage streetcar sites you can visit.

Starting in the east on the outskirts of Montreal at Saint-Constant, Quebec, you will find at least 13 former Montreal streetcars starting with #350 (The Rocket), built in 1892. Sixty-four years later, in 1956, #350 was completely refurbished and can be seen at the Canadian Railway Museum there and is now 122 years old. Like all transit museums in Canada, at Saint-Constant there are always one or two streetcars to give rides on a mile or two of track.

Ontario has the largest Canadian streetcar museum. They have over a dozen streetcars and some interurbans that operate over a mile and a quarter of double track. The Halton County Radial Railway Museum is situated between Guelph and Rockwood, approximately 50 miles from downtown Toronto. It has been in operation since 1954 when volunteers had two streetcars donated to them from Toronto Transit. After that, they had to buy land, scrub out bush, acquire rails and build a roadbed for them. Over the next 45 years, dedicated enthusiasts built three or more barns to house the streetcars, moved a station from Rockwood to their site, and built a $100,000 reception area that features a large area for books, videos, and souvenirs. Light lunches are also available. A few students are hired for the summer months to work in the lunch and souvenir area, but other times the work is handled by volunteers.

Calgary, Alberta has two running streetcars from the 1910 era. They operate from the station in Heritage Park to one of the parking lots at the edge of the park—about one-half mile. You will also find a replica of an 1882 Winnipeg horsecar in that same park. Until a few years ago a horse was used to pull it on a track to give people rides. It is the only car like it in Canada. Winnipeg was the farthest western city to operate horsecars (1882-'94).

Edmonton, Alberta has the main heritage streetcar museum in that province. There are seven operating streetcars that run in Fort Edmonton Park in the summertime as needed. Three are former Edmonton city cars, one dating all the way back to 1908 when streetcars first commenced in that city. The other two were brought in from Toronto and rebuilt. In another area of Edmonton they have that more cars that run over the High Level Bridge. One of these cars was built in Japan in 1921 and ran there until 1990—nearly 70 years. It was brought over to Edmonton in the early 1990s and started operating over the bridge in 1995. The second car, built in 1946, came from Melbourne, Australia in 2004. Most recently, a third car has been acquired from Saskatchewan. All of these cars are double-end, so no loop is needed at either end to turn around. The driver just changes the location of his steering by walking from one end of the car to the other when they reach the end of the line. He then commences his return trip from that opposite end.

In the past few years the track has been extended from the Strathcona area of Edmonton to downtown Jasper Street. Volunteers have done nearly all of this work.

In other cities, Vancouver runs two interurban cars— #1207 and #1231. These cars were built in 1905 and 1912. They ran into the mid-1950s—in fact, these streetcars, along with two others, made the final ceremonial run from Steveston on February 28, 1958. The last car to enter the barn that day was #1231, ending 67 years of interurban service. When operations ended, these cars were sold to a museum in the United States. Some years later, they were bought back and with some government and private money and many dedicated volunteers they were refurbished and #1207 began operation in 1998, running along a track from Granville Island. In 1999 #1231 joined #1207. There is also a wooden streetcar, #53, built in the early 1900s. It is situated in the Spaghetti Factory restaurant at 53 Water Street in Vancouver. The car is set up with tables and chairs for lunches. There is an additional interurban car, number #1220 that can be found in storage in Steveston, south of the Vancouver airport.

Chapter Nineteen

NELSON, B.C. SHOWS HOW IT'S DONE

Nelson B.C. in the southeast Kootenays region of the province is a prime example of people coming together to accomplish a vision. A community of volunteers came together to resurrect the streetcars and they were able to run once again. The B.C. Government granted the city a reasonable sum of money for the project on the stipulation that for each dollar the government supplied, the city had to come up with an equal amount of dollars. This amount would be gained not only through various fundraising efforts, but, where physically possible, the construction and building of the car and track had to be completed by dedicated volunteers. This was quite an accomplishment given that Nelson B.C. is a relatively small community.

Nelson had streetcars in operation for 50 years, from 1899 to 1949. Like other cities, the cars were stripped and sold at the end of service in 1949-'50. One of these, #23, an original wooden car from Cleveland, Ohio, was built in 1906 and brought to Nelson in 1924. It operated in Nelson until 1949. After sitting outside for nearly 35 years it was brought back to the city in 1984. Over the next six years it was completely refurbished with 40 percent original product and 60 percent new material.

Streetcar #23 in Nelson, B.C. is very similar in shape to the older wooden Winnipeg streetcars; author photo.

The owners of the railway that runs through Nelson donated the rails and helped lay them. Electricians established the overhead trolley wire. A barn was built to house the car and a small substation was erected to supply the power. Six years after work began on the project, the grand opening was held July 1. 1992. Streetcar #23 ran along the edge of Nelson by Kootenay Lake on two kilometers of track. In the first two months of operation it carried 20,000 passengers. Volunteers operate the streetcar and the fares charged bring in enough revenue to cover daily expenses.

The car has run every summer since and is a great tourist attraction. They are also restoring a Birney streetcar #400 that ran in Victoria for a number of years from 1921 to 1948. It was initially stripped down and used as a bunkhouse before being retrieved some years later and rebuilt.

The most surprising feature of all this community participation is the fact that the City of Nelson is a community of only 10,000 people. In contrast, Winnipeg, with a population well over 700,000 cannot accomplish a similar

OUR FORGOTTEN HERITAGE

achievement with our streetcar in waiting, #356. Several reasons are put forward when this fact is mentioned. It's very hard to get parts for a car built 105 years ago. True, but how do heritage sites in Canada and the US find parts for their cars? Canada has six working heritage streetcar sites. The US. has at least 38 active sites, some with a couple of streetcars, some with several dozen. If parts weren't available from some source, these cars wouldn't be running. Some of these heritage sites have streetcars stored on the property but haven't the money or time to rebuild them. It's possible these owners may be willing to sell some of the parts require to refurbish #356.

Edmonton obtained streetcars from Japan, Australia, and Toronto. Vancouver bought two of their early 1900s interurbans back from museums in the US. They now run in Vancouver on summer weekends. Belgium even donated a complete streetcar to Vancouver. It arrived in September 2000.

Europe still operates streetcars in many of their cities. The streets are too narrow to accommodate the thousands of cars it would require to carry the millions of people the streetcars do. The Netherlands, Germany, Switzerland, Italy, France, and Poland, are a few of the European countries that operate streetcars in some of their cities. The Netherlands, Germany, Switzerland, and Austria, have heritage streetcars that range from 50 to 90 years old. Communication with these heritage sites could lead to finding some of the necessary parts to refurbish the Winnipeg car. But, you also need finances. There lies another obstacle.

Chapter Twenty

WHERE ARE OUR FINANCIAL SUPPORTERS?

It is amazing how money appears when some group or someone with genuine interest gets involved financially to see a worthwhile project get completed. When the Canadian Museum of Human Rights was proposed, millions of dollars came forth before drawings were completed. The Royal Bank building on Main Street attracted a million plus for renovations. Several hundred thousand dollars are being considered to beautify a block-long stretch of Century Street in St. James to entice visitors to our city to take that route downtown on their way from the airport.

A dedicated group of mostly retired railroad men raised $350,000 to rebuild the old steam boiler on their 1882 steam engine that pulls the Prairie Dog Central Railway steam train on weekend excursions in the summertime.

In the millennium year of 2000 the Canadian government set aside money for each province for a project that would recognize the past, be in step with the present, and harmonize with the future. One idea that would have fit that requirement would have been to rebuild the streetcar and have it on track at The Forks site. It could have helped to manage pedestrian traffic by making a 20 minute round trip from The Forks to the Exchange district and back again. Car #356 was built here in 1909 and operated on the streets of Winnipeg for 46 years until the final days in September 1955—significant in the history of the city. It has been waiting 60 years in its lonely vigil as the only car left from the original 400 to get its day in the sun. Rebuilding it would take care of the present. Once back on track again it could run in limited service for another 45 years, thereby having been involved with our history for 140 years. As other cities have found out, streetcars are good tourist attractions and pleasantly present history to those of the younger generations.

Instead, the city chose to repair and refinish the Golden Boy that sat on top of the Legislature for the previous 80 years. Granted, the statue's body needed some surgery to repair a few minor dents and a complete exterior finish to bring the gold coating back to its original brilliance. A special scaffold was built on the dome to be able to reach and remove the Golden Boy, and the statue spent about five months being renewed and then placed back on the dome again. It apparently cost $7 million to complete this project. The Golden Boy did not arrive in Winnipeg until 1919. By that date the city had already had streetcar service for 37 years and electric service for 27 years. From 1921 to 1925—in just four years—the streetcars carried 235 million passengers and traveled a total of 36 million miles, which equals 1,440 trips around the world, without one fatality during that time. They took citizens to work, to the parks for picnics, to church, sporting events, shopping, and visiting relatives and friends, and extended that service outside the city with trips to Selkirk and Stonewall. The streetcars were a major factor in promoting the city's growth because they provided good reliable service to the outlying areas of the city.

OUR FORGOTTEN HERITAGE

In contrast, some may ask - what has the Golden Boy done for Winnipeg other than entice questions from tourists wondering, "What he is, who he is, and what is he doing up there?" He is even too high to be able to appreciate the fine work of the sculpture. But the difference is he is out there and can be seen, whereas the streetcar is invisible, and that's the main problem—out of sight, out of mind.

Chapter Twenty One

ONLY TEN OF THE HERITAGE BUILDINGS WERE HERE BEFORE THE STREETCAR

As just mentioned, part of the problem that challenges the issue of getting support for a streetcar restoration project is the invisibility of the Winnipeg streetcar. At the tourist bureau at The Forks there are pictures or models of old City Hall, the Prairie Dog Central Railway, bison, fishing scenes, fur traders, dog teams, farm tractors, sport items, and models of statues you would find at the entrance to several different Manitoba towns. But, you will not find a picture or model of a Winnipeg streetcar. Unless one has been added lately, the same situation applies to the Manitoba Museum at Rupert and Main Streets. It's hard to understand why the streetcars are not even hinted at after a historical existence of three quarters of a century in the city.

In contrast, more of the tall buildings downtown, built mainly between 1895 and 1905, are receiving Heritage Status. The tall buildings with their fancy cornices, arched windows, and exterior statues, display the excellent workmanship done by the tradesmen of that era, in contrast to the cement slab and sheet of glass styles in which present-day structures are assembled. The advantage these buildings have is they are seen by the passing public and their image is impressed on the mind, whereas the streetcar of that era is nowhere to be seen. Furthermore, most of the buildings will still be around 50 years from now, but will that situation also apply to the streetcar?

To illustrate: walking tours of Winnipeg's heritage buildings are conducted each year on a weekend in May. Approximately 70 of the city's heritage structures are available to inspect. It would be impossible to see them all in one weekend, so people choose the areas they are most interested in and have time to see. They range from the well-known government and city buildings to houses of the early pioneers and businessmen, cathedrals, and churches over a century old. But what is not emphasized is the fact that 60 of the almost 70 heritage buildings on this tour to promote our heritage history were built after the streetcars arrived in 1882. Fifty of those 60 buildings were built while the streetcars were here, and before the first four buses arrived in 1918. Only 14 were constructed in the 1800s:

- St. Boniface Museum (1845)
- Seven Oaks Museum (1851)
- Kildonan Presbyterian Cemetery and Church (1852)
- St. James Assiniboine Anglican Church (1853)
- Ross House Museum – First Post Office (1854)
- St. James Museum (1856)
- St. Norbert Provincial Park and House (1871)
- The Occidental Hotel (1873)
- Bleak House (1873)

OUR FORGOTTEN HERITAGE

- Riel House National Historic Site of Canada (1881)
- Vaughn Street Jail (1881)
- Holy Trinity Anglican Church (Donald and Smith, 1883)
- Wesley Hall, later the University of Winnipeg (1895)
- Dalnavert Museum home on Carlton Street (1895)

The horsecars arrived in 1882. One could surmise that the easy transporting of the citizens by the streetcars in the downtown area, greatly influenced where the buildings were located. Unfortunately, this part of our heritage history seems to be overlooked. In future tours it would be nice to see some recognition of the role that the streetcars played in making it more convenient to reach these buildings, many that are now over 100 years old. This could be done by visiting car #356 in the Via Rail museum or providing some printed literature that would inform those on the tour that the streetcars played a big part in the development of Winnipeg's heritage.

In 1882 Winnipeg's population stood at 8,000 people. By 1901, it had reached 52,000. Forty-two streetcars carried 3.5 million passengers that year. This was before the arrival of the automobile and 18 years before transit buses started operating. The public streetcars provided the transportation necessary to facilitate the moving of people to the services that they needed. In everyday life, without options for commuting, population growth would have suffered. With increased population comes the need for buildings to host provision of these services.

At this point, what Winnipeg needs most is a dedicated group with the desire and ability to put in motion a streetcar rebuilding program—first to refurbish the car and then bring forth a plan to run it at The Forks. One day, hopefully in the not too distant future, the citizens of Winnipeg could look back proudly at their accomplishment and become the seventh Canadian Heritage Streetcar City to have an car operating every summer.

If nothing is done to rectify this in the next five years, it looks like #356 will have finally reached the end of its line. The few streetcar operators who are left will be in their mid and late 80s to mid-90s and another era, the final one with regard to Winnipeg streetcars, will come to an end. In 2023 Winnipeg will be celebrating its 150th anniversary. Having #356 refurbished and operating would be evidence of the historical significance that the streetcars have provided to the early growth of the city.

In the final analysis, perhaps two well-respected men of that era, Walter E. Bradley from the Winnipeg Electric Street Railway and Gordon Sinclair Sr. from the *Winnipeg Tribune* said it best. On September 19,1955, these two men combined their talents to write a final column in the *Winnipeg Tribune* about the demise of the streetcars.

"And so it is on Monday when the north Winnipeg car house doors close behind the last streetcar, they will be just as surely closing an era 73 years long—an era in which Winnipeg grew from a small town on the banks of the Red and Assiniboine rivers to a mighty city—grew because the streetcar was there to open streets and highways, industrial locations, suburbs and parks. Quieter buses will replace them, but the clang of the gong, the rattle of the wheels, the "swoosh" of the released air, the flashing of the trolley poles will long be remembered."

I can't think of a better example of how the presence of the streetcars (here for 23 years before Eaton's opened their store in 1905 providing major employment for the citizens of Winnipeg) was a major cog in the growth of the population from 68,000 in 1905 to 175,000 in 1918.

OUR FORGOTTEN HERITAGE

We all know someone who worked at Eaton's, especially new immigrants looking to get a start in new surroundings in Winnipeg. Eaton's store was the biggest company in western Canada.

If the streetcars had not already been here Eaton's wouldn't have built here--they would have had to wait 13 years, from 1905 to 1918, for the first buses to bring customers to their store. But the streetcars could bring people from several areas of Winnipeg, and from 1908 even bring them from Selkirk, Manitoba. By 1925 there were still only 25 buses.

They would have been kept pretty busy carrying the population, in the 200,000 range by that date. So, because of the start that the streetcars gave the Eaton's store, Winnipeg was able to keep it there for nearly 95 years. No wonder every one knows someone who worked at Eaton's, and stayed and raised a family too!

Personally, I'd be perfectly happy to be back on the old streetcar again, watching down the track on a frosty winter morning hearing the groan and whine of the motors as the car picks up speed from its last stop. You can hear it first, and then you see it in the distance sporting that bright orange front (not the anemic white our present buses are saddled with) that can be mistaken for a furniture truck in the distance. As it comes closer you see the trolley sparks as it hits the overhead contacts and occasional switches. Pulling into the stop, the operator fans the breaks a couple of times and you hear the hiss of the air and can see it mixing with the early morning winter frost. Next, you hear the squeaky rattle of the front door opening to receive you, and just as you board, the throb of the compressor begins building the air that was used the last couple of stops back up to the required 80 pounds pressure. The operator releases the air break with a loud hiss, the front door slams shut and with a couple of taps on the gong, the motors whine and sing out as they pick up speed clattering over the joins in the track like you hear you hear on railway coaches. Inside, the lights flicker now and then as the trolley wheel passes through the contacts. The process keeps repeating and in no time we are downtown. Hey – I think I'll get off at Eaton's!

Whoops, we are not living in that world anymore—it's back to reality! Maybe someday, if I live long enough, they will restore #356 and we could have a similar ride in it.

Like our youngest grandson used to say, " Bring it on!" Hey I'd settle for that any day.

As I, too, am reaching the end of the line, I couldn't have said it any better myself.

REFERENCE INFORMATION

FACTS ON 73 YEARS OF WINNIPEG STREETCAR SERVICE

1882 HORSECARS 1894

- YEARS 1882 – 1894 TOTAL OF 20 CARS
- BUILDER JOHN STEPHENSON COMPANY NEW YORK
- CONVEYANCE WOODEN CAR PULLED BY HORSES ON RAIL LINE
- OUT OF SERVICE 1894

1891 (Jan) ELECTRIC STREETCAR SERVICE (Sept) 1955

- Total years of operation - 64 years
- 27 years before the first 4 City buses came into service in 1918, And 10 yrs. before our City's first automobile arrived in 1901

TOTAL NUMBER PRODUCED

YEARS	BUILDER CONVEYANCE	CONVEYANCE	OUT OF SERVICE	TOTAL NUMBER PRODUCED
1890 - 91	PATERSON & CORBIN CANADA	4 WOODEN CARS	1937 – 2 CARS	OTHER 2 EARLIER 4
1892 – 93	OTTAWA CAR COMPANY	5 OPEN CARS 14 CLOSED	1920 – 29	19
1897 – 1906	TORONTO RAILWAY COMPANY	4 OPEN CARS 56 CLOSED CAR	1937 – 39 3 USED UP TO 1955 REMAINING WERE REBUILT	60
1904 – 1908	OTTAWA CAR COMPANY	31 WOODEN CARS	1918 – 25 REBUILT TO 1200 SERIES AND 1400 SERIES CARS	31
1903 – 1907	WINNIPEG STREET RAILWAY	7 OPEN CARS 43 CLOSED CARS	ALL UNTIL 1939 3 – LASTED TO 1955 MOST STAYED 1948 - 54	50
1908 – 1909	WINNIPEG STREET RAILWAY	36 WOODEN CARS CLOSED	1954 – 14 TAKEN OUT OF SERVICE 1955 – 22 TAKEN OUT OF SERVICE	36

OUR FORGOTTEN HERITAGE

YEARS	BUILDER CONVEYANCE	CONVEYANCE	OUT OF SERVICE	TOTAL NUMBER PRODUCED
1910 –1911	WINNIPEG STREET RAILWAY	64 WOODEN CARS	1920'S – 8 TAKEN OUT 1940'S – 19 TAKEN OUT 1954 – 18 TAKEN OUT 1955 – 19 TAKEN OUT	64
1912	WINNIPEG STREET RAILWAY	32 WOODEN CARS	1940 – 14 TAKEN OUT 1952 -54 18 TAKEN OUT	32
1913 –1914	WINNIPEG STREET RAILWAY	62 WOODEN CARS	1920'S – 4 TAKEN OUT 1940'S – 21 TAKEN OUT 1952 – 54 – 34 TAKEN OUT 1955 – THE LAST 3 TAKEN OUT	62
1919	OTTAWA CAR COMPANY	20 STEEL CARS	RAN TO END OF SERVICE 1955	20
1920	TWIN CITY RAPID TRANSIT COMPANY	20 WOOD CARS SECOND HAND, REBUILT IN WINNIPEG	USED TO 1950	20
1921	PRESTON CAR AND COACH COMPANY	5 STEEL BIRNEY CARS	USED MINIMALLY UNTIL 1946 THEN SCRAPPED	5

THE STREETCARS OF WINNIPEG

YEARS	BUILDER CONVEYANCE	CONVEYANCE	OUT OF SERVICE	TOTAL NUMBER PRODUCED
1924	WINNIPEG ELECTRIC COMPANY	7 REBUILT CARS TO 1200 SERIES	USED UP UNTIL 1939 THEN SCRAPPED	7
1925	WINNIPEG ELECTRIC COMPANY	21 REBUILT CARS TO 1400 SERIES	USED UP TIL 1939 THEN SCRAPPED	21
1928	WINNIPEG ELECTRIC COMPANY	1 STEEL STREETCAR # 798 –LONGEST STREETCAR IN CANADA	USED UNTIL 1955	1
1929	WINNIPEG ELECTRIC COMPANY	1 STEEL STREETCAR # 796 –NEWEST AND LAST CAR	USED UNTIL 1955	1

- TOTAL NUMBER STREETCARS 433 - (274 BUILT IN WPG.)

- Provided employment for thousands of workers over 73 years of dedicated service

1908 INTERURBANS 1939

- INTERURBAN CARS BUILT IN WPG TO SERVE STONEWALL & SELKIRK MAN

- 1908-1911 2 coaches, 6 trailers, and 4 combination baggage coaches each 60 feet long

- OVER THE 60 YEARS WINNIPEG USED 15 sweepers, rotary plow, sand cars, sprinkler car, Rail grinding cars, Derrick Crane cars, wrecking car, and several flat hauling cars.

Glossary of Transportation Units

PCC STREETCARS

A number of presidents of US and Canadian streetcar companies held a conference to try and design an improved, streamlined streetcar that could be manufactured by different companies. They were mass-produced—that way they would fit into the format of other cities cars (except for color) if one city reduced their streetcar fleet and another city was wanting to buy more. In 1934-35 they developed a type of car that all companies could obtain. They were called the "Presidents' Conference Cars," hence PCC. From 1935 on most cars were of this model. Toronto had 744 of them in their transit system.

HORSECARS

They inaugurated streetcar service in Winnipeg in October 1882. They looked like a smaller, old-type electric streetcar. They were about 20 feet long and could seat about 10 or 12 on each side. They traveled on a rail track and were pulled by one or two horses.

About 20 horsecars and 80 horses served Winnipeg from 1882 until May 1894. Winnipeg was the most westerly Canadian city to operate horsecars.

DOUBLE-END STREETCARS

These streetcars looked exactly the same from both ends. Inside there was a metal five-foot high controller column with a gear handle. When engaged it would move the car ahead or back. Therefore, the motorman of the car could operate it from either end. It didn't need a rail loop to turn the car around. When they reached the end of the line the operator just walked to the other end and the rear became the front. These cars needed two trolleys, one at either end, but only one was used at a time. The active one was always at the rear. The other one was stored in a bracket on the roof. They stopped building double-end cars about 1906 as more rail loops were used.

TWO-MAN CARS

A two-man car had one door at the front and double doors at the rear. The operator, sometimes called the motorman, controlled the movement of the car and the conductor at the rear opened and closed the double doors and watched the fare box, took and gave out transfers when necessary, and sold tickets. Passengers boarded and left the car by these rear doors. When it was really busy the motorman might open the front door to let people out or occasionally open the door for a customer he knew had a monthly pass, because the operator carried no tickets, change, or transfers.

ONE-MAN CAR

As the title says, only one man, the operator, was in this car. Some of these cars had double front doors so passengers could board through one door and leave by the other. The majority of the older wooden cars only had one front door. These cars were all equipped with a steel treadle step at the rear door. When the operator remotely activated the treadle step the weight of the person standing on it opened the door. If no one else was leaving the car, the door would shut after that person left. The operator had to sell tickets, make change, and give and receive transfers, basically doing all the things the conductor used to handle. This system started in 1924, thereby eliminating the wages of the conductor.

MASTER FRONTS

Nine cars were built with a master fronts after being in accidents. They had a wider slanted front window and narrow corner windows, which gave the operator a little better view from the front. It also made the cars look a little more streamlined.

A BIRNEY STREETCAR

These were a shorter, stubby kind of car and they were double-enders. Five of them arrived in Winnipeg in the early 1920s to run on the short lines but were used very little and were stored by the beginning of the 1930s.

SWEEPERS

Winnipeg had 16 sweepers; actually four of them were rebuilt ones after being damaged in the major streetcar barn fire in 1920. A few were larger for heavier snow. The majority were a bit smaller to handle some of the tighter curves in the rail loops. Two men operated them much like an electric streetcar—one was the operator while the other handled the depth and angle of the wide, revolving bristle brushes.

ROTARY PLOW NO. 18

For severe winter snowstorms especially in the Headingley, Selkirk, and Stonewall areas, this plow would tackle the 10- and 12-foot snowdrifts on the line and blow them off the track. Then the sweepers might follow in a cleanup mode.

SPRINKLER CAR

Opposite of the snowplow, this sprinkled the dusty streets with water in the summertime.

SAND CAR

This was usually a retired wooden streetcar that was equipped to pour sand on the rails to make a quicker stop, just as salt or sand are used on the roads today when they get slippery. Sand was also used in the fall when sap from the trees would drip on the rails, which could make the wheels on the streetcars go for a slide.

SERVICE CAR OR WRECKING CAR

This was also an older car equipped inside with various tools if a streetcar had been in a collision. This vehicle would travel down the track and try to repair it enough to return to the barn. If possible they would hook on to it and tow it back.

DERRICK CARS

They had a couple of these electric cars. These were used them for lifting or laying rails, Rails weighed 90 pounds a lineal yard so a 10-foot rail would weigh near half a ton. Also, if a streetcar had been badly damaged they might need a derrick car to pick up the pieces and then tow in what was left.

LINE CAR

A regular service truck with a rising platform that could rise nearly 20 feet if needed to reach the 600-volt overhead lines that supplied power for the streetcars and electric trolley buses. The truck was needed to install switches, replace lines, and make repairs. Usually two men, sometimes three, would be needed on the line truck.

INTERURBAN CARS

The interurban cars operated on rails just like the streetcars. They were mostly 60 feet long, about 15 feet longer than a streetcar. On a straight, firm track they could travel 50 miles an hour. They were fitted with a baggage section that often was used when they brought cream, milk, and garden produce from Selkirk and Stonewall into Winnipeg. They operated from Winnipeg to Selkirk from July 1908 to September 1937 and from Stonewall from December 1914 to May 1939. In the 1920s they made eight to11 round trips a day. In 1923 they carried 1,196,000 passengers to these two towns. Their presence during that time helped the growth of these towns immensely.

HEADINGLEY LINE

Two smaller 37-foot interurbans ran from Higgins and Main to Headingley from December 1905 until May 1930. Like the other interurbans, they also carried farm products to Winnipeg.

Streetcar Bulletin Public Service News May 1925

DESTINATION AND STREETCAR ROUTE NUMBER SIGNS.

NO. 2. Any car turning around Garry Loop from any point in the city will bear this number.

NO. 3. Cars from the north operating via Logan avenue, Princess, Donald, and Terminating at Donald and Broadway.

NO. 4. Cars operating from the south via Donald, Princess, Logan around the CPR Loop.

NO. 5. Cars from the north making their terminus at Donald and Portage Ave.

NO. 6. Cars from the South operating via Main Street to the CPR Station.

NO, 8. All cars operating other than those described in numbers 4 and 6, making the CPR Loop their terminal.

NO.17. Cars operating on Portage Avenue West to City Limits. (St. James Street)

NO.20. Cars operating north on Main Street to the North Car House.

NO.21. Cars operating west on Portage Avenue to Deer Lodge loop.

NO.22. Cars operating north on Main street to North City Limits. (McAdam Avenue)

NO.23. Cars operating west on Portage Avenue to Victoria street, or cars connecting at Deer Lodge with cars to Victoria Street.

NO.25. Cars operating west on Portage to Deer Lodge connecting with cars operating to St. Charles.

NO.26. Cars operating north on Main street to Templeton avenue.

NO.29. Cars operating west on Portage avenue connecting at Deer Lodge with cars to Headingly.

NO.32. From Broadway and Donald East on Broadway, North on Main to Redwood Bridge, Hespeler Street to the end of Morse Place Line. (Watt & Munroe area.)

NO.35. From Elmwood via Louise Bridge, Higgins, Princess Donald, Broadway, Sherbrooke, Maryland Bridge, Academy Road to Doncaster Street.

NO.36. From Union Station west on Broadway, North on Donald Princess, Logan, North on Main street, via Redwood Bridge to John Black Church.

NO.37. From Elmwood via Louise Bridge, Higgins, Princess, Donald, Broadway, Sherbrooke, Maryland Bridge, Academy Road to Assiniboine Park.

NO.38. Follows route number 36, connecting at John Black Church with cars to East St. Paul.

NO. 39. Follows route no.35, connecting at Doncaster wye to Charleswood car.

NO.40. All cars making their destination Sutherland and Higgins.

NO.42. All cars making their destination Talbot and Stadacona.

NO.44. From Doncaster wye, Academy Road and the reverse of route 35, to the End of the Elmwood Line at Talbot and Roland.

NO.51. All cars to Union Station and main Car House at Assiniboine and Main.

NO.52. Cars from Garry Loop over Provencher Bridge, south on Tache, east on Marion, north on Des Meurons, west on Provencher to Garry Loop.

NO.53. All cars whose destination is Tache and Marion.

NO.54. From Garry Loop, Provencher Bridge, South on Des Meurons, west on Marion, north on Tache to Garry Loop.

NO.55. South on Main Street to the junction of St. Mary's and St, Anne's Road.

NO.56, From St. Mary's or St. Anne's Road, North on Main Street, west on Dufferin, to Dufferin and Arlington.

NO.57. South on Main Street to end of St. Anne's Road Line via Norwood Bridge and Main Street Bridge.

NO.58. North on Main Street from St. Mary's or St. Anne's Roads to Mountain, West on Mountain to Mountain and Arlington.

NO.59. South on Main street to end of St. Mary's Road Line via Norwood Bridge and Main Street Bridge.

NO.71. From Garry Loop west on Sargent to Dominion Street.

NO.73. From Garry Loop west on Sargent to Valour Road.

NO.75. From Garry Loop west on Notre Dame to Wall Street.

NO.77. From Garry Loop west on Notre Dame to Keewatin Street.

NO.80. Corydon Ave, east on Portage, south on Main, west on Broadway, south on Osborne, west on Corydon, north on Lilac, west on Grosvenor, north on Stafford, via Maryland Bridge, north on Sherbrooke, east on Portage Ave.

NO.81. The reverse of NO. 80.

NO.87 All cars bound for south Car House & Buses operating on Morley Avenue.

NO.89. All cars operating south on Osborne street to River Park.

NO.90. North on Osborne, East on Portage, north on Main, west on Selkirk, north on McGregor to Luxton (North Car House)

NO.91. Following route NO.89, with destination Elm Park.

NO.92. North on Osborne, east on Portage, north on Main Street, west on Selkirk to Selkirk and Sinclair.

NO.93. Following route NO 91 to Parker Avenue.

NO.95. Following Route NO.93. Connecting with cars at Parker Avenue operating to The Junction of the St. Norbert and Agricultural College Lines.

NO. 96. North on Osborne, east on Portage, north on Main street, west on Selkirk to Mc.Phillips.

NO, 97. Same as Route NO.93. Connecting at Parker Avenue with cars to Agricultural College.

OUR FORGOTTEN HERITAGE

NO.99. Same as Route NO.93 to Parker Ave. with cars operating to St. Norbert.

POPULATION OF CITY OF WINNIPEG

DATE	POPULATION
1870	215
1871	607
1872	1,467
1873	1,869
1874	3,000
1875	5,000
1882	7,985
1884	20,000
1891	25,000
1900	40,000
1901	52,000
1904	67,262
1911	136,000
1913	150,000
1921	170,870
1931	218,785
1946	307,494
1972	505,000
2000	650,000
2008	694,668
2013	714,000 *source Dafoe (see references)

OUR FORGOTTEN HERITAGE

Where are they now?

Streetcar (number unknown) used for storage south of Winnipeg; Steven Stothers photo.

Streetcar #356 as it sits today at the Canadian Railway Museum; Steven Stothers photo.

Streetcar #680 resting north of Winnipeg in a cow pasture; Steven Stothers photo.

Streetcars in a row on a farm in southern Manitoba; Steven Stothers photo.

OUR FORGOTTEN HERITAGE

Streetcar located in southern Manitoba; Steven Stothers photo.

REFERENCES

Archives of Manitoba Photo Collections

J.E. Baker Photo Collections

J.E. Baker, Winnipeg's Electric Transit: The Story of Winnipeg's Streetcars and Trolley Buses. Railfare Enterprises Ltd. Toronto 1982. ISBN 0-919130-31-3

W. E. Bradley, A History of Transportation in Winnipeg, MHS Transactions, Series 3, 1958-59.

Dafoe, C. Heart of the Continent, Great Plains Publications 2002.

H.W. Blake, The Era of Streetcars in Winnipeg 1881 to 1955. Winnipeg 1971.

H.W. Blake, The Era of Interurbans in Winnipeg 1902 - 1939. Bishop Printing, Winnipeg 1971.

Library and Archives Canada Photo

OUR FORGOTTEN HERITAGE

<u>Moving with Winnipeg Since 1882</u>, Public Service News Booklet Centennial Issue October 1982; (20 page booklet).

G. Sinclair Sr. ,The Winnipeg Tribune Newspaper, September 17, 1955.

Steven Stothers Photo Collections

Winnipeg Transit Photo Archive Collection

Last streetcars going through Portage and Main September 19, 1955; Winnipeg Transit Photo Archive Collection.

The author is reunited with #692 in 2012.

About the Author

My parents immigrated from Northern Ireland to Winnipeg in the summer of 1927. I was born in November 1928. I was an only child. It was the start of the depression years and jobs were scarce. As a 4 year old I remember riding the streetcar downtown with my mother. If I behaved while she shopped at Eaton's she would take me to the Woolworths store and buy me a 10 cent toy! By 1933 my father couldn't obtain any kind of work in the city, so we moved to a vacant farm about 100 miles west of Winnipeg in the district of Keyes. My parents, city slickers, knew absolutely nothing about farming but we survived. I attended a one room school. One teacher taught all the subjects from grade one to 10. There were never more than 20 to 25 kids in the whole school. We had no radio for 3 years, no car for 7 years, no electricity for 16 , no telephone for 10 and never did have running water or plumbing. In 1954, I left the farm at the age of 25. I became employed by Winnipeg Transit for the next 38 years. The girl I had been dating also moved to Winnipeg and we were married in 1955. We have 2 married daughters,4 grand children and 1 great grandchild. I retired August 1st 1992 after 38 years driving streetcars, trolley buses, and diesel buses, was the last streetcar employee to retire. From badge 825 to badge 1.

Printed in Canada